Contents

Foreword

Mr Martin Burr has written this short book so that health visitors can readily refer to the various legal considerations which may arise during their work. As in all text books the opinions expressed are the author's own and are intended to be guidelines rather than definitive legal answers. I can commend Mr Burr's book as a valuable guide and I hope that it will prove useful to many health visitors.

All of us whatever our job or profession work within a legal framework. This is true of health visitors who work within the community giving primary health supervision and advice especially for mothers and young children. Inevitably from time to time they will meet situations which involve legal problems. In such circumstances it is important that they seek advice from the legal departments of their own professional association or of their health authority or from a private solicitor.

Health visitors should not regard the law as a straitjacket but as a support. Doubt about the law must never inhibit action which health visitors from their professional training and experience know is required. Sometimes they will encounter an emergency, for example a young child seriously uncared for. In such a situation the health visitor should not hesitate to take appropriate action. Delaying to find out what the law is could endanger the child. In such situations the health visitor can rightly assume that the law and the courts will be supportive.

London
September 1982   *Michael Morland*

Preface

This is a short book. It attempts much. It seeks to be a brief exposé of English law as it affects the health visitor practising in England and Wales. It seeks to expound the law in simple and readable English. I hope it will also show that the law does have a rationale and can be interesting, even fun. But it is by no means an exhaustive treatment and is thus no substitute for the advice of the Health Visitors' Association or a professional lawyer. It will, I hope, help you to know when you need such advice, and to understand that advice in a new and clearer light. I try to keep my clients out of court, rather as you try to keep yours out of sickness. I hope this book will help you, and provide enjoyable reading, even if it cannot always keep you out of court.

Finally I would like to thank all those who have helped in whatever way, however small, to bring about this book, but particularly Michael Morland, Esq, QC; Mrs Jane Wyndham-Kaye, OBE, Barrister-at-Law, Miss D Wall, MSSCh, MBChA, FSSCh; Michael Collins, Esq, MA(Oxon), MPhil; C N Jordan, Esq, MA(Oxon), of Middle Temple, Barrister-at-Law, Senior Court Clerk in the Middlesex area of Greater London for reading all or part of the manuscript and removing a myriad of "misprints"; my parents and Mrs Diane Allard for doing so much to accelerate the final preparations of the manuscript; Mrs Diane Jardine for retyping the manuscript so elegantly; A P Andrews, Esq, MA, Principal Law Lecturer and Adviser SW Thames RHA; and Mr Brian Edsall, my publisher, for his patient understanding, help and guidance.

So long as the health visitor is in the land of the living the law of this realm holds sway. You need not and should not walk in darkness where the law is concerned. I hope this short book will place some beams of light and a few quips of fun along your path. Perhaps the Coroner's Court is "but the gate of life immortal". But whether it is or not, it is to be hoped the health visitor will now stand in a greater light – that is at Law!

The law is stated in the light of materials available on 1 March 1982.

CHAPTER 1

ENGLISH LAW AND THE
ENGLISH LEGAL SYSTEM

1. The Common Law: The administration of justice in England and Wales today stretches back to William the Conqueror. The common law, which forms the basis and backbone of English law and the English legal system, is the body of law created, then developed by the Royal Judges from the Norman Conquest to the present day. From the thirteenth century these judges sat basically in three courts, Exchequer, Common Pleas and King's Bench. Since the Judicature Acts 1873-75 they have sat in the High Court, the Court of Appeal and the House of Lords. The common law is so called because in medieval times it was the law common to the whole realm, as distinct from local customary laws on which it to some extent drew and which it gradually replaced. These customs only applied to particular localities and originated in Anglo-Saxon times. Nowadays the term "common law" tends to be used as distinct from other forms of law, notably Statute law.

2. Precedent: The cornerstone of the common law is the doctrine of precedent, which means that once a case has decided a particular point of law, that decision must be followed in all subsequent cases involving that point of law, unless a higher court overrules it. Decisions of the House of Lords, which is the highest court in the land, bind all other courts, though not necessarily the House of Lords itself. Decisions of the Court of Appeal bind all other courts except the House of Lords, just as a decision of a High Court judge binds all lower courts and tribunals but not the Court of Appeal nor the House of Lords, nor another High Court judge. Decisions of courts lower than the High Court, and tribunals do not constitute precedents in England and Wales. However, decisions in other countries with the common law system (e.g. USA and Commonwealth countries such as Canada and Australia) do create precedents which are regarded as "persuasive authority". Thus an English or Welsh court is not bound to follow the judgement of such a case, but if there is no English or Welsh authority it may well be persuaded so to do. Some Commonwealth countries (e.g. Singapore and Trinidad and Tobago) still have appeals to the Privy Council, whose decisions are theoretically "persuasive authority" only, but since the judges of the Privy Council are drawn from the House of Lords and the Court of Appeal, they are very persuasive indeed.

In spite of the importance of the doctrine of precedent, a judge may say that the facts of a particular case are different from those of an earlier case claimed as precedent and can apply a different rule of law. Nevertheless cases decided by the courts are crucially important for anyone who wishes to obtain even a simple working knowledge of the law and how it functions in England and Wales.

3. Equity: Parallel to the common law there developed a body of law called "Equity". In medieval times the common law did not always do justice, sometimes because the defendant was so powerful that the jury was intimidated, sometimes because the common law was too inflexible to provide a cause of action, sometimes because it could not give an adequate remedy. So people petitioned the King who in time referred the matter to the Chancellor. Then the petitions came to be addressed to the Chancellor sitting in the Court of Chancery. At first equity "varied as the length of the Chancellor's foot", but by the nineteenth century it had developed a clear-cut system of rules and precedents. Since the Judicature Acts of 1873–75, both common law and equity have been administered by the same courts, although the two systems remain distinct, and to this day the rule first established by James I still prevails and where common law and equity conflict, equity prevails.

Equity (literally "fairness") supplements the law and mitigates its rigour. Only equity sets aside transactions because of "undue influence" and in recent years it has been used to protect the rights of wives and others with no legal interest in their homes, it is the foundation-stone of trusts, and it was equity that first developed the rule that an employee cannot be compelled to work for an employer.

4. Statute Law: The great advantage of precedent is that once established the law is certain thereafter. But there are drawbacks. The law can become too rigid and find difficulty in embracing new fields of human activity. Also established precedents, and even a particular decision, may sometimes displease the government of the day, whether that government be medieval barons, the leaders of a modern political party or something in between. So that ever since Anglo-Saxon times there has been written law or legislation, enacted at first by the King in Council, and later by the Crown in Parliament. Since about 1800, legislation (i.e. written Acts of Parliament) has made most of the fundamental changes in the law, and many areas of English and Welsh law today, including that relating to medicine and nursing, are almost entirely statutory, and contained in written Acts of Parliament.

Under English law Parliament is sovereign, and can make or repeal whatsoever laws it wishes. The courts can and do interpret the Statutes (or Acts) which Parliament passes, and what is called the case-law thus generated is often crucial in knowing what the law of England is. For example, Section 1 of the Abortion Act 1967 includes a requirement that the pregnancy be terminated by a registered medical practitioner. In the case of Royal College of Nursing of UK v. DHSS [1981] A.C. 800 it was decided in the House of Lords that the induction/prostaglandin method, which has a very high level of nurse involvement, did not offend the requirement.

5. Delegated Legislation: Much modern legislating is done by delegated legislation, which means that Parliament delegates its authority to a named person or body which it empowers to make legislation. For example, Local Authority by-laws and regulations are a form of delegated legislation, as are the Rules of Court, which are contained in two separate books and are the rules of procedure and evidence for the High Court and the Court of Appeal on the one hand, and the county court on the other. Most delegated legislation comprises the rules and orders made by ministers and by the Queen in Council, and these are called Statutory Instruments.

Although an English court cannot declare an Act of Parliament void and of no effect, it can declare a Statutory Instrument *ultra vires*, i.e. "beyond the powers" of the person or body making it and thus void. In recent years the courts have been particularly zealous to resist any attempts by the executive wing of the Government to amass great power in its own hands through the use of Statutory Instruments.

6. European Community Law: Britain is now a member of the European Economic Community, certain parts of whose laws are directly applicable here without the intervention of Parliament. In some circumstances an individual may be able to rely on Community Law before an English court.

Doctors, dentists and nurses now have free movement throughout the European Community, and midwives will have from January 1983. Directives for pharmacists are proposed, but at the time of writing (March 1982) none are proposed for health visitors.

7. Text-Books and Lawyers' Caution: Acts of Parliament and reports of cases take a long time to read and can be difficult to understand. A good text-book will give the reader a working knowledge of a particular area of the law, but the law is contained in statutes and decided cases, not in text-books, and text-book writers' opinions are not law.

Even when a professional lawyer has looked up all the relevant statutes and cases, the law may still be uncertain, just as the medical profession is not omniscient about disease, and great scientists often eschew claims to omniscience. The proverbial "lawyers' caution" is thus rooted in prudence, wisdom and experience and is not the product of a nervous disposition. Besides, lawyers never know what facts will emerge in due course, particularly if they put a client into the witness box.

8. English Courts: Like most legal systems, English law is divided into criminal law and civil law. Criminal law is a branch of public law and deals with conduct which constitutes a criminal offence, for which the offender may be prosecuted and, if found guilty, punished. Civil law deals mostly with the rights and duties between one citizen and another. Sometimes these rights and duties are general legal obligations, like not trespassing on one's neighbours' land by having a picnic in their front garden, not committing a nuisance by allowing one's weeping willow to overhang the fence of their back garden, and not interfering with their right of light by erecting a garden shed which prevents the sunshine permeating their sitting-room windows. Transgressions are called "torts". Alternatively these rights and duties may be agreed between the parties and thus arise under a contract e.g. buying a railway ticket or goods in a shop. Sometimes these rights and duties are a matter of the law of real property (i.e. land law) e.g. whether A or B owns Blackacre and whether C, the next-door neighbour, can take short cuts through the back garden of Blackacre, because there is a right of way.

At the lower levels, different courts administer the two types of law.

CRIMINAL COURTS

a. Magistrates' Courts: 95 per cent of criminal cases are dealt with in magistrates' courts. In rural areas usually three lay magistrates who are neither paid nor legally qualified, sit on the Bench and are assisted by the Clerk to the Justices, who is usually a qualified lawyer. In London, and other big cities, as well as lay magistrates, a stipendiary (salaried) magistrate who is legally qualified, sits alone. Magistrates have two principal functions, firstly to hear the less serious criminal cases and secondly to "commit" the more serious ones for trial at the Crown Court.

Since the Criminal Law Act 1977 there have been three types of criminal offence: (a) those triable summarily (i.e. by magistrates only); (b) those triable on indictment (i.e. by the Crown Court only); and (c) those triable either way. (a) includes the less serious offences such as exceeding the speed limit, and driving without due care and attention. (b) includes all the more serious ones such as murder, rape, arson and robbery. (c) includes offences such as minor shoplifting where the accused has the right to trial by judge and jury in the Crown Court, but can consent to be tried by the magistrates. But under (c), if the magistrates think that their powers of sentence are inadequate they can commit the accused to the Crown Court for sentence. Magistrates also have limited civil jurisdiction, e.g. as licensing justices for liquor and gaming, and important powers in matrimonial and family matters (especially care proceedings – see p 49).

The juvenile court, which deals with persons under 17, is a part of the magistrates' court. Its sittings are in private and only the magistrates, court staff, the parties, parents, legal representatives, witnesses and the press are present. The press must not disclose facts which might lead to the identification of the accused or the accused's address or school. The procedure in the juvenile court is rather less formal than in an ordinary magistrates' court.

b. Crown Courts: The Crown Court deals with the more serious criminal cases. Here the accused is tried on indictment (i.e. when formally charged) by a professional judge sitting with a jury. On the most serious cases (e.g. murder) a High Court judge normally sits, and on the less serious ones (e.g. burglaries, shoplifting) a Circuit judge, or a part-time judge called a Recorder, normally sits. On appeals from magistrates' courts a professional judge sits with two or more lay magistrates.

Since 1972 the twelve men and women who sit on the jury are drawn from a random cross-section of society. Everyone on the electoral roll aged under 65 is liable to be summoned for jury service and must attend, unless they are exempt. Those exempt include peers, members of Parliament, barristers and solicitors, practising medical practitioners, dentists, nurses, midwives, veterinary surgeons and practitioners, pharmaceutical chemists, and criminals. It is

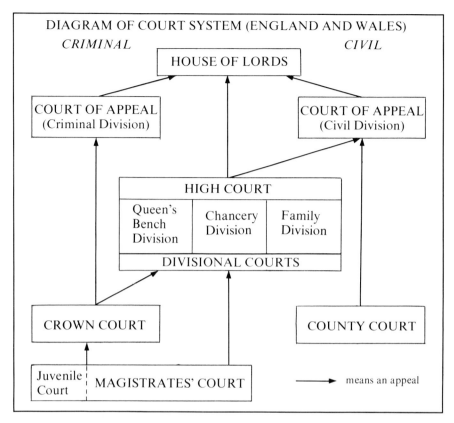

DIAGRAM OF COURT SYSTEM (ENGLAND AND WALES)

CRIMINAL   CIVIL

HOUSE OF LORDS

COURT OF APPEAL (Criminal Division)

COURT OF APPEAL (Civil Division)

HIGH COURT

Queen's Bench Division | Chancery Division | Family Division

DIVISIONAL COURTS

CROWN COURT

COUNTY COURT

Juvenile Court | MAGISTRATES' COURT

⟶ means an appeal

not clear if health visitors are exempt through being qualified nurses. Apparently jury summoning officers have no set policy on this point. So if you are summoned you can either serve, or argue the point with the jury summoning officer.

The Crown Court was established by the Courts Act 1971 to replace the Assizes and Quarter Sessions which had existed since medieval times, and unlike the old Assizes and Quarter Sessions, the Crown Court has jurisdiction over offences committed anywhere in England and Wales, its jurisdiction not being confined to a particular locality, as magistrates' courts are. However, the locations at which the Crown Court sits are divided into six Circuits.

CIVIL COURTS

A civil action can either be brought in the county court, or in the High Court. In some matters the county court has exclusive jurisdiction (e.g. under the Rent Acts, which protect leasehold residential accommodation). But generally its jurisdiction is limited. The limit for claims relating to a contract or a tort (wrong doing) is at present (1982) £5,000. If the claim is below that it should be brought in the county court, if above that in the High Court. The county court also has limited jurisdiction in matrimonial and family matters (see pp 52–56).

Unlike the Crown Courts, each county court has jurisdiction only for a particular area, while the High Court, like the Crown Court, has jurisdiction throughout England and Wales, and sits mainly in the Royal Courts of Justice in the Strand, London.

The High Court is divided into three divisions, Queen's Bench (dealing with contract, tort, commercial law, etc.), Chancery (dealing with trusts, wills, conveyancing, certain aspects of mental patients' property, company law, tax, etc.) and Family. The last is the most important to health visitors as it deals with divorce, maintenance, custody of children, access to them and wardship matters.

The Court of Protection is an Office of the Supreme Court (i.e. the High Court and the Court of Appeal) comprising the Lord Chancellor, three nominated judges (drawn from the Chancery Division), a Master and a Deputy Master. It protects and manages the property of patients under the Mental Health Act 1959. It is assisted by the Lord Chancellor's visitors (one lawyer, three doctors and ten lay visitors).

From both the High Court and the county court, appeal lies to the Court of Appeal and thence to the House of Lords.

Circuit judges sit in the county court, whilst in the High Court, High Court judges sit. In both, however, what lawyers call interlocutory matters, which are simply preliminary discussions about a case before the full trial, are dealt with by Masters in the Queen's Bench and Chancery Divisions, and by Registrars in the Family Division and the county court. Masters and Registrars hear cases in Chambers and not in open court, and press and public are not admitted.

THE LEGAL PROFESSION

The legal profession in this country is divided into two branches, barristers and solicitors. Barristers are either QCs (Queen's Counsel) who are the most senior barristers, or juniors (which is all other barristers). The public have no direct access to barristers, who are called "counsel", and have to go through a solicitor, who "briefs" counsel, which means preparing the papers in the case which are sent to counsel tied in red tape, hence the expression.

Only barristers can argue cases in all higher civil courts, but solicitors can, and often do, argue cases in magistrates' courts and county courts. They also have limited rights of audience in the Crown Court. Some barristers specialise in court work, and are called common law barristers who deal with crime, divorce, personal injury work like road accidents and industrial injuries, etc. Other barristers are Chancery barristers and specialise in drafting legal documents, dealing with trusts, wills, conveyancing, company law, tax, and so forth.

Every major case which comes to court is presented by a barrister, and it is a barrister who drafts the concise statements of the facts on which each party relies and which are called the pleadings. Many civil cases are, however, settled out of court, about 99 per cent in personal injury cases.

CHAPTER 2

THE HEALTH VISITOR IN COURT

In the last chapter we looked briefly at English law and the courts which administer it. Now we must consider what happens when the health visitor, perhaps for the first and only time, comes face to face with the law and its administration, as a witness in court.

In January 1975 the Health Visitors' Association issued the following:

Recommendations concerning the involvement of
health visitors in court proceedings

1. Health visitors have no rights of entry and the success of their work therefore depends entirely on their ability to win and retain the confidence and trust of the families they visit. Consequently, a publicised appearance as a witness in court proceedings of any kind can have seriously damaging effects.

The Association's first and main recommendation, therefore, is that health visitors should be protected from any professional involvement in court proceedings at all, except when evidence which only they can give is essential in the interests of justice.

2. Experienced health visitors report that, after a publicised court appearance, the loss of confidence in their discretion will be somewhat reduced if they can explain to other families that they had been legally compelled to give the evidence in question. Accordingly, the Association's second recommendation is that health visitors whose evidence is shown to be essential should always be permitted to insist on a subpoena.

3. Bearing in mind the primary object of protecting health visitors, whenever possible, from the need to appear in court at all, the Association advises its members that they should report immediately to their Nursing Officer if they are asked for a statement of facts by social workers, solicitors, parents or even the police, informing the enquirer that, as officers of the Health Authority, they are not permitted to make any statement without authorisation.

4. The Association then recommends that a health visitor should have both professional advice from her Nursing Officer and legal advice from a Legal Officer both before and during the making of the statement so that she can be helped towards avoiding any further involvement whenever possible.

5. When a health visitor is served with a subpoena to give evidence which has proved essential, the Association recommends that she be given an opportunity to discuss her evidence in advance with a Legal Officer so that she fully understands what will be expected of her and what is permissible, e.g. possible reference to relevant case notes and a request to be excused from answering publicly a question which would involve a serious breach of professional confidence.

6. When a health visitor is particularly disturbed and anxious about the ordeal of giving evidence, the Association recommends that she be given an opportunity, a day or two before her evidence is due, to spend a short while in the public gallery of the court in which she will have to appear in order to familiarise herself with procedure and atmosphere and that, when she goes to give her evidence, she be accompanied by a Nursing Officer or a colleague health visitor.

7. If a health visitor is required to give evidence at an inquest and there is any possibility of her work being called in question in any way, the Association recommends that she be supported by a Legal Officer.

It is strongly recommended that health visitors study these and then look them over again when a court appearance first becomes a real possibility.

The purpose of a health visitor's call at a house is to promote the health of the family living there, especially the children and an expectant or nursing mother, and to offer the hand of friendship. It is not to gather evidence for court proceedings and it should not be so used subsequently. But there may be special cases where the interests of the child or the family in question require the health visitor to give evidence in court.

What happens if the subpoena arrives?

1. Trial by ordeal: Once you have received a subpoena you must attend at the time and place stated, even if you have other and important commitments. Failure to do so is punishable as contempt of court. If you are ill, telephone the court and the solicitor calling you and then write a letter of confirmation to both.

Any public appearance is something of an ordeal for anyone. Health visitors in court are no exception. Think what actors go through before every performance. Often those at the top of their profession develop the most hyperactive adrenal glands. Remember that even counsel questioning you, whether an eminent QC or a raw junior, will be at least a little tremulous.[1] Even judges are not immune.[2] Lord Pearce once said that the judge appears "to float along on the Bench with effortless serenity like a swan on the mirrored surface of the lake". But, his Lordship reminds us, "the judge, like the swan, is paddling madly underneath".[3] Remember finally that many other health visitors have been through just this ordeal and survived!

The Health Visitors' Association, as has been seen above, recommends that health visitors who are particularly worried about the ordeal of giving evidence should be allowed to spend a while in the public gallery of the court where they are to appear, a day or so beforehand, to find out what happens. It also offers courses which include mock trials or "moots". Both these forms of practical experience are used by law students and are strongly recommended.

---

1. Remember that in some courts solicitors can conduct cases – see p 14.

2. In this chapter what is said of judges applies to magistrates and, often, coroners (but see Chapter 5).

3. Quoted Megarry, *Judges and Judging* (Child & Co. Lecture 1977).

2. Before your appearance: There are many tips one can give any witness before a court appearance.

Never arrive late if you can possibly avoid it. Lateness annoys judges, and it will hardly endear you to the other parties to the litigation either. And it will ruin your all-important equanimity. Remember that counsel are expected to arrive half an hour before the court sits or (if a specific time is allocated) before their case is due. Be sure in advance you know how to find the court building and are suitably dressed.

From your nursing training and experience you will know the advice to "relax", a valuable tip which is easily forgotten, particularly on your first court appearance. Remember also that you are a professional person, so you must stand up straight and act like one. Say in your own words what you believe to be so. Do not exaggerate and be consistent.

The most important advice is, "speak the truth" and "do not lose your head". A truthful witness can never be tripped up. We all make mistakes, but if you keep your head and think carefully both before going into court and before answering each question when you are in the witness box, you will help minimise the risk. Always listen carefully to the question you are asked and answer that one and not the question you hoped to be asked! We all forget things too, and courts and counsel are used to both, and practice will help avoid them. Be sure your papers are in order and refresh your memory from your statement, case notes or other records at least the day before the hearing. A calm, clear, truthful and firm witness is an impregnable fortress to the most devastating cross-examining counsel. The root of this is integrity, the watchword of all professional people, but to bear fruit it needs self-confidence plus authority and control (in the medical sense of those terms), and your pre-trial reports and statements (civil or criminal) must be of the same standard.

There is one last tip. Your first appearance in court is likely to be the worst ordeal, but after that it should become easier, perhaps still something of an ordeal, but less so. Think of the first time you handled a patient on your own.

3. At court: You arrive at court. You have come in answer to a subpoena. The first thing to do is to ascertain in which court your case is being heard. In provincial magistrates' and county courts there is often only one court sitting, which is always so for Coroners' Courts. In Crown Courts and in magistrates' and county courts in London and other big cities there are often two or three. In the Royal Courts of Justice in the Strand there are over fifty. In the Old Bailey there are twenty-five.

You should know the title of your case and the name of the court in which it is to be heard. These will be on your subpoena. In civil cases the title will be in the form <u>Smith v. Jones</u> (pronounced "Smith *and* Jones") where Smith is the plaintiff (i.e. the person bringing the action) and Jones is the defendant (i.e. the person against whom it is brought). In criminal cases the title will usually be in the form <u>R. v. Jones</u> (pronounced "The Queen against Jones" in court and "Regina versus Jones" outside), where Jones is the person accused of the crime. For minor offences the title will often be <u>Smith v. Jones</u>, where Smith is

17

the police officer bringing the prosecution. Sometimes (including care proceedings – see p 49) you will meet the form In the Matter of Smith (or In re Smith).

It is important to know in which court your case is being heard, firstly because it bears directly on the nature of the case in which you are to give evidence, and secondly because, particularly out of London, Crown Court, county court and magistrates' court are often in close proximity. Thus if you arrive at the wrong one the solicitor calling you will be hunting everywhere for you and *vice versa*, both unsuccessfully. You might even be arrested for contempt, but this does not usually happen! The different courts and their work were discussed in Chapter 1.

If you have any difficulty finding the appropriate court, one of the court officials will be pleased to assist. They are easy to recognise, because ushers wear a gown while other court officials usually wear a uniform or badge of some sort. Remember that a solicitor conducting a case in the county court also wears a gown, but wears tabs (i.e. bands) as well, while counsel wears a wig in addition to gown and tabs. Generally in a magistrates' court, no-one wears robes (i.e. gown etc.) except the ushers. Often there is an enquiry desk at the entrance to the court building.

Outside each court you will find a list giving the name of the court, the name of the judge and the titles of the cases to be heard that day. This list will tell you when your case is expected to be heard. Normally courts sit at 10.30 a.m. (sometimes 10.00 a.m.) and rise at 4.15 p.m. (4.30 p.m. for criminal courts). The luncheon adjournment is usually from 1–2 p.m. In the Royal Courts of Justice a list called the "Daily Cause List" is published each evening listing the cases being heard in every court there the next day.

Now you must make yourself and your whereabouts known to the solicitor calling you or, failing that, to one of the court officials. This is important for various reasons. For example, it would be rather awkward if you were called to give evidence while you were having coffee in a nearby café. Again, one pupil barrister had once to search everywhere for the chief witness who turned out to have been sitting quietly in court throughout. You should always bring your subpoena with you, by the way.

In criminal cases witnesses must generally remain outside court until called to give evidence. This is to prevent them hearing what previous witnesses have said and adjusting their evidence accordingly. In civil cases this sometimes applies, but generally witnesses are allowed to sit in court throughout. However, this is a matter for the judge, and you must abide by any ruling the judge makes. Perhaps the most sensible course in the first instance is to ask the solicitor calling you where to wait when you arrive. Remember that the wait may be a long one, and sometimes at the very last minute your evidence is not needed, perhaps because the defendant pleads guilty (criminal cases) or the case ceases to be contested (civil cases) or simply because counsel decides not to call you.

4. Your evidence: Once you begin giving evidence, you must under no circumstances talk at all to anyone else actually involved in the case, and not even to anyone not actually involved about the case. This applies until you have finished giving evidence, and is to prevent your evidence being in any way influenced. This means standing apart while waiting for the court to sit, going home on your own when the court adjourns for the day, and lunching on your own. This rule can be relaxed when appropriate. For example, if the court adjourns while you study a long document, counsel calling you may ask leave of the judge and of counsel on the other side, to inquire whether you are ready to resume giving evidence. But you must always observe the rule unless the judge gives special permission to relax it.

Also you must never go home until either the case concludes, or the court adjourns for the day, or the judge discharges you for that day, for instance because your evidence will probably not be reached before the next day. Normally counsel calling you will ask for your discharge if appropriate.

When you have finished giving your evidence, you must wait at the back of the court until either the case is over or you are discharged by the judge. This is in case you are recalled to give further evidence. Again counsel calling you will normally ask for your discharge if appropriate.

If your evidence seems unlikely to be called on a particular day, or your evidence is finished, and you need a discharge for some other engagement, you should ask the solicitor calling you to ask counsel to obtain leave from the judge. Of course, the more warning you can give the better.

When the time comes for you actually to give your evidence, counsel will say "Call" and then your name. This will be repeated outside court if that is where you are. Go quietly to the witness-box, and an usher will be there to ensure you reach the right place. First you must take the oath. The usher will give you a New Testament or other appropriate religious book, which you hold in your right hand. You then repeat the words of the oath which are normally printed on a card, but if the court does not have one, you will be asked to repeat the words after an officer of the court, usually the Clerk to the Court or the Registrar. The normal formula is "I swear by Almighty God that the evidence I shall give shall be the truth, the whole truth, and nothing but the truth" (in juvenile courts "I promise before Almighty God . . ." etc.). If you have no religious belief or oath taking is contrary to your religious belief, or for some other reason you object to taking an oath, you can tell the usher and you have the right to make a solemn affirmation. But you should be clear that the affirmation is just as binding in law and on your conscience as an oath. The formula for an affirmation is "I do solemnly, sincerely and truly declare and affirm that the evidence I shall give etc."

Now you can give your evidence. Counsel calling you will question you first. This is called "examination-in-chief". You will be asked three formal questions. First, your full name, second your address (the court will usually accept your professional address, if you do not wish to disclose your home address, though it can insist on it), and third your occupation. As a rider to the third question counsel may ask how long you have been a health visitor. These three questions should help put you at your ease.

Now comes the body of your evidence. Do not volunteer information, but wait to be asked questions. Always address your answers to the judge. Forms of address for judges are contained in Appendix I, but do not worry if you make a mistake, as it is easily done and most judges are used to this and, provided you are polite, do not mind. Remember how the Princess-of-Wales-to-be purported to marry Philip Charles Arthur George. However, it is more professional and gives you confidence if you can address judges correctly. Always speak slowly and distinctly, so that everyone can hear what you say. Remember that the judge will take a note of your evidence and will be anxious not to miss a point on which the whole case might turn. The judge may ask you questions, even while you are being examined by counsel, but usually this will only be if something needs clarifying.

Do not be afraid of using medical terms. Lawyers who deal regularly with medical matters have a copy of *Black's Medical Dictionary* on their shelves and are familiar with its contents. If you do floor them, they can always ask you to elucidate. Do so in simple language, and do not spout jargon. There is a difference between technical terms and jargon.

When you are being examined-in-chief, counsel will couch questions in the form "What was the condition of the baby when you visited?" This is because counsel in chief must not ask "leading questions", which are questions which give an indication of the answer they expect. If, for example, counsel asked "Did the baby have severe lacerations on the arms?" that would imply that you are expected to answer "Yes" and counsel would be prompting you. As part of the essence of a fair trial is to attempt to ascertain the truth, the court must have *your* evidence and not what counsel prompts you to say.

For the most part you need not worry about the rules of evidence which are the problem of judge and counsel. Your job is to tell the truth and to answer questions fairly and accurately. But remember such rules exist, and if you find counsel "editing" your evidence, this is probably to steer you away from prejudicing a fair trial by inadvertently giving inadmissable evidence. Indeed this is one reason why counsel has your written statement, which lawyers call "proof of evidence", the other being that without your written statement counsel would not know what to ask you or what you are going to say. It is you who witnessed the events in question, not counsel.

Finally there are two rules of evidence which you must know. Firstly, in criminal cases the general rule is that the jury must not know that an accused person has previous convictions. This is because the accused must be tried on the evidence given on this particular occasion and not on previous events, so anything which suggests previous convictions is generally inadmissible.

Secondly, in criminal cases, and to a lesser extent in civil ones, the general rule is that you cannot tell the court what someone else told you, unless you are merely giving evidence that the statement was made and not that the statement was true. For example, if the mother tells you the father beat the child, you can give evidence of the bruising you found on the child because that is what you yourself saw, but you cannot tell the court what the mother said, because she was not on oath when she said it and was not cross-examined on what she said. However, you can give evidence of the father's explanation of the bruising if, say, it was unsatisfactory and that is why you reported the matter, because what counts there is what the father said, not whether what he

20

said was true. This is called the rule against hearsay evidence. This, like all rules has its exceptions, which are for council and judge to worry about. Just remember that it is this rule which makes council stop you saying something which would break it, and which applies when you are preparing your evidence.

When counsel calling you has finished, you will be cross-examined, when counsel for the other side will ask you questions about what you have said "in chief". This is to test the evidence you have given and to put the other side's case so that you can comment. Passing this test will give it much more weight. Some health visitors have unfortunately had a rough ride in cross-examination and it can be disconcerting to have your opinions questioned if you are not used to it. But never take counsel's questions personally or as a personal slight on yourself or your integrity. They are not meant that way, and if they were or if counsel asks an improper question, the judge will intervene. Remember, the other counsel must represent the interests of that counsel's client, for whom your evidence may have serious, perhaps very serious, consequences. As a professional person, cross-examination will probably be less of an ordeal for you than for an ordinary witness, but even so counsel may have to suggest that you made a mistake or to question your opinion. If a client instructs counsel, so and so is my case, then that is what counsel must put to you. Remember the old adage "There are two sides to every argument". Unlike examination-in-chief, in cross-examination you *can* be asked leading questions (i.e. those suggesting the expected answer) and these can be difficult to answer. But if, for example, counsel suggests an injury was not very serious, do not just agree or disagree, keep calm and say in your own words how serious you thought it was.

If you are a witness for the plaintiff or the prosecution and there are several defendants they may be represented by separate counsel who all have the right to cross-examine you. If one counsel represents more than one defendant you may be asked some questions on behalf of one defendant and some on behalf of another.

After you have been cross-examined, counsel calling you may ask you questions on what has arisen in cross-examination. This is called "re-examination" and is usually very short. Its purpose is to put the record straight if necessary. After that, unless the judge has any further questions, you leave the witness-box and hopefully your ordeal is over. But remember not to leave the court without a discharge from the judge or until the case ends, and remember your nursing training regarding "sag-lag", i.e. after an ordeal.

5. *Using records:* While giving evidence, you are not allowed to use the written statement given to your counsel or, in legal terms, your "proof of evidence". The court wants to hear what you remember of the events in question, not what you said to someone else about them in the interim. But there is no rule of law which prevents you refreshing your memory from your written statement or otherwise before you go into the witness-box, provided, of course, that the evidence you give is the truth, the whole truth, and nothing but the truth as you yourself honestly believe it to be. (Remember that when

21

you make a statement to the police, or anyone else, you should always keep a copy.) If you are a prosecution witness in a criminal case and you refresh your memory thus, the defence should be informed by those calling you and you may be cross-examined about this, because it may affect the weight which can properly be attached to your evidence.

The rules about written documents are varied but it will probably meet most needs of the health visitor if these are simplified into two categories.

a. Contemporaneous record: You may refer in the witness-box to any record or other document which was made by you or under your supervision, provided it was made either at the same time as the events referred to or very shortly thereafter.[4] This exception should enable you to use your personal case notes, memoranda and the like to refresh your memory. It may also enable you to use reports and records which you have made if they are sufficiently contemporaneous.[5] Normally the court will leave you in possession of your case notes, but (and this has happened) if you do use your case notes to refresh your memory, you must, if requested, disclose any document so used to the other side or their counsel, as well as to the judge and to the jury if any, and you may also be cross-examined on your notes etc. too. This may raise problems of confidentiality (see below), but it should be remembered that it may be very difficult for counsel on the other side to cross-examine you fairly without seeing a document of which the accuracy may be crucial, and we have discussed the importance of cross-examination previously.

If for any reason you are not willing to disclose a document, you cannot refresh your memory from it, nor can you give evidence based on what it says without bringing it with you and producing it in court. You can only answer from your own recollection, which you may find difficult if, for example, you made several visits so that you cannot recall each one precisely and your evidence may well be impaired in consequence.

If you are going to produce a document in court you must normally produce the original because experience has shown that copies are not always reliable. But if you can say on oath that you actually remember the events referred to in the document and need to refer to it merely to refresh your memory, then a copy will probably do.[6]

The crucial point is that your oral evidence must be based on your

---

4. What constitutes "very shortly thereafter" is a "matter of fact and degree" for each case: R. v. Simmonds (Appendix II). The crucial point is, were the facts still fresh in your memory when you made the record? Decided cases suggest that up to about one month is in order: R. v. Fotheringham [1975] C.L.R. 710 where the Court of Appeal disregarded a gap of twenty-two days; cf and contrast R. v. Graham [1973] C.L.R. 628 where the Court of Appeal on the facts was doubtful about a gap of one month. It is recommended, however, that the sooner your notes are written up the better: if you can do it the same day, you should.
5. Even if such reports and records are not sufficiently contemporaneous in themselves, you may still be able to use them if they are compiled from case notes or the like which are sufficiently contemporaneous and the report or record in question is substantially a transcript of or contains substantially what was in the case notes or the like: R. v. Cheng (Appendix II); Horne v. Mackenzie *(ibid)*.
6. Where the "copy" amounts to a transcript see above.

recollection or on what you wrote down when the events were fresh in your memory. If you are in doubt, you should consult a Legal Officer or seek other legal advice before you go into court, but under no circumstances can you use a memorandum drawn up for you by a legal adviser.

b. Reports: Sometimes a report you have written is tendered in evidence in its own right, and the other party in the case wishes to cross-examine you on it. If so, the report itself will be available to counsel for both sides, to the court and to yourself. Otherwise the rules outlined above apply. As you have seen (pp 15–16), the Health Visitors' Association recommends that health visitors seek advice from their Nursing Officer and a Legal Officer both before and during making any statement, to help avoid further involvement wherever possible. But whatever advice you may receive, your report must be a truthful and accurate statement of what you believe to be so, must be written in clear, simple and lucid English (if you find this difficult, you should do something about it), and must be the work of a professional person such as yourself.

Finally remember that if you are using National Health Service records in court, you must always have the permission of your superiors and the higher the better. The NHS is most insistent that its records must not be used in court without official permission.

CONFIDENTIALITY

The question of giving evidence in court and particularly that of using records in court leads naturally to the issue of a health visitor's professional confidence which involves medical and nursing ethics and matters of law.

As a matter of medical and nursing ethics, the cardinal rule which governs all members of the medical and nursing professions will already be well known to every health visitor. All matters appertaining to a patient's private life are very, very strictly confidential unless there is a medical record which is freely available anyway. If patients consent, you may speak for them where it will help them, but even then only medically and only to medical and nursing colleagues and to them alone. You may not speak against a patient. And you may never, even to professional colleagues, under any circumstances discuss what has been related to you privately.

By virtue of the multi-disciplinary nature of their work health visitors sometimes encounter confidentiality problems, and the Health Visitors' Association has issued the following eight-point code on confidentiality to which reference should be made and with which all health visitors should be familiar. This code should resolve any problems which arise, but if not, then you should consult your professional body.

Guide for health visitors on confidentiality

1. As a general rule, the best method of sharing confidential information is a small case conference at working level or a personal meeting with the other worker involved. Any record or recommendation from the case conference should be circulated only to members of the conference and under confidential cover.

2. No confidential information should ever be passed on until the identity of the recipient and the use to be made of the information have been confirmed.

3. Health visitors should never pass on medical details to anyone. Their response to such requests should always be to recommend reference to the general practitioner or consultant concerned.

4. When a client actually specifies that information is given in the strictest confidence, the client's permission should always be obtained before the information is passed on except in special circumstances such as the prevention of crime or of detriment to others.

5. Health visitors' records should record separately factual information suitable for passing on to those who need and who are entitled to receive it, and social and personal information not to be passed on unless it is really required for the client's benefit. School records should also be in two parts, medical information being separate from the information to be available to the school.

6. Correspondence intended to be confidential ought to go unopened to the addressee. In order to ensure this, health visitors and their clients should be advised to mark the envelope "Strictly Confidential".

7. In court proceedings a client's confidences are privileged only if made to a solicitor. If a health visitor is asked a question the answering of which would be a breach of professional confidence, she should ask the Judge or the Magistrate if she can either be excused from answering or be permitted to answer in private. If this request is refused she has done all she can and has no option but to answer in open court.

8. Health visitors should accept responsibility for ensuring that all staff working with them understand and respect the confidential nature of their work.

In practice the courts try to respect medical and nursing confidentiality when possible, and medical and nursing witnesses are frequently protected because they are not pressed to disclose matters which would breach their professional confidence, and judges have discretion to disallow questions.

Finally what happens if you are served with a subpoena requiring you to produce in court some of your documents and records? You should immediately seek legal advice to preserve confidentiality. You must under no circumstances ignore the summons, and unless you can challenge it successfully, it is essential that you do what you are required to do. In one such case there was an immediate appeal to the Crown Court where the judge accepted at once that health visitors' case notes were confidential and need not be produced in evidence.

CHAPTER 3

THE LAW SURROUNDING
THE HEALTH VISITOR

In the last chapter we tried to prepare you for the experience of a court appearance. In this chapter you can return to your clinic. What is the legal framework surrounding you and your profession?

Up to 1979 responsibility for the education, training, registration and professional conduct of the nursing and midwifery professions was delegated by Parliament to the General Nursing Council on the one hand, and the Central Midwives Board on the other. Both were given powers equivalent to those exercised by the General Medical Council in relation to registered medical practitioners. Health visiting was regarded as coming within the responsibility of the General Nursing Council, even though health visitors were required to have a midwifery qualification as well as state registration for nursing.

In 1962 Parliament set up the Council for the Education and Training of Health Visitors to supervise health visitor training and education and to issue Health Visiting Certificates. Disciplinary matters, however, continued to be the responsibility of the General Nursing Council.

In 1979 all previous arrangements governing the education, training, registration and conduct of the nursing, midwifery and health visiting professions were replaced by the Nurses, Midwives and Health Visitors Act[1] which set up the United Kingdom Central Council for Nursing, Midwifery and Health Visiting, with National Boards for England, Wales, Scotland and Northern Ireland, which replaced the General Nursing Councils, the Central Midwives Boards and the Council for the Education and Training of Health Visitors. The United Kingdom Central Council was empowered to maintain a register of qualified nurses, midwives, and, for the first time, health visitors, to determine by means of rules approved by the Secretary of State for Health and Social Services the education and training requirements and other conditions for admission to the register, the prescribed training courses being provided by the National Boards. The Central Council was given the responsibility of regulating the professional conduct of those on the registers including investigation of alleged misconduct and the issuing of sanctions subject to an appeal to the High Court. The majority of the maximum of 45 members of the Central Council are nominated by the National Boards in equal numbers, the remainder being appointed by the Secretary of State for Health and Social Services. There will be a special Midwifery Committee as a standing committee of the Central Council.

The maximum numbers on the National Boards will be 45 in England,

---

1. At the time of going to press the Act has been passed but is yet to be implemented. The dates for implementing the various parts of the Act are decided by the Secretary of State.

Wales and Scotland and 35 in Northern Ireland. At first all members were appointed by the Secretary of State but in due course the majority will be elected. Most members of both the Central Council and the National Boards will be nurses, midwives or health visitors. There will be a Midwifery Standing Committee of each National Board and a Health Visiting Joint Committee which will also be a standing committee. The Central Council and National Boards must consult this committee on all health visiting matters and the majority of its members must be practising health visitors. Local training committees may also be established.

Anyone wishing to have their name on the register must satisfy the Central Council that they are of good character and have the appropriate professional qualifications for a nurse, midwife or health visitor. This means that they must either have undergone training in the United Kingdom and passed examinations required by the Central Council's rules, or be a national of an EEC country holding a professional qualification from it and designated by the Secretary of State as being equivalent to British requirements, or finally have undergone, outside the United Kingdom, training which is recognised by the Central Council.

In law, therefore, the licence to practise health visiting is granted by the Central Council for Nursing, Midwifery and Health Visiting and the education and development of the profession is finally determined by it, acting on the advice and recommendations of the Health Visiting Joint Committee. Disciplinary powers, however, are in the hands of the Central Council from whose judgements an appeal to the High Court can be made.

While the Central Council, through its various subsidiary councils, is responsible for the professional aspects of the health visiting profession, practising health visitors are the employees of the National Health Service which was created by the National Health Service Act of 1946. This came into operation in 1948, since when the service has been re-organised twice and currently operates under the National Health Service Act of 1977, which was itself amended by the Health Services Act 1980. Responsibility to Parliament for the working of the service rests in England with the Secretary of State for Health and Social Services, and in Wales with the Secretary of State for Wales. The civil service departments which administer the NHS are the Department of Health and Social Security (DHSS) for England and the Welsh Office for Wales.

With the exception of general practitioners, all members of the medical and nursing professions who work within the NHS (including health visitors) are employees under a contract of service. Their employer is the Health Authority, not the DHSS.

There are advisory committees at national, regional and district levels which Health Authorities must consult, and provision is made for Community Health Councils. These are watchdogs at district level and consist of 20–30 members, half appointed by local government councils and the rest mostly by voluntary bodies interested in the local health services. They have access to the Health Authorities, the right to secure information and the right to visit hospitals.

There are two Health Service Commissioners (one each for England and

Wales) to investigate complaints from the public. Complaints can only be considered if they are first sent to the appropriate Health Authority, and actions taken solely in the exercise of clinical judgement and the actions of GPs are outside the Commissioner's jurisdiction. The Commissioner reports annually to the relevant ministers who lay the report before Parliament.

THE LEGAL RIGHTS OF THE HEALTH VISITOR

Although health visitors are in Crown service, they are not civil servants, and are not regarded as Crown Servants for most purposes of the Employment Protection (Consolidation) Act 1978, so they have the full rights of any ordinary employee except that their entitlement to redundancy pay is covered by a quite separate Whitley Council agreement, which also gives them the same rights to minimum notice of dismissal as the 1978 Act. Also the Act gives no right to written particulars of their contract, though in practice the NHS always supplies these.

What rights does the law accord the health visitor on duty? The main rights you are likely to need to know in practice fall into two categories: (1) as an employee of a Health Authority; and (2) if you are injured on duty.

The corresponding duties will be dealt with later.

The Health Visitor — an Employee

a. Contracts of Employment: As a health visitor you are an employee of a Health Authority. There is a contract between you by which you are both bound. Its precise terms can be crucial, particularly if there is a dispute e.g. about the hours you work or the work you do. Your rights and duties and your employers' are governed primarily by that contract, but also by certain common law rules relating to contracts of employment and the employment legislation passed largely during the last decade and now contained in the Employment Protection (Consolidation) Act 1978 as amended by the Employment Act 1980.

This is a rapidly developing area of the law. Much legislation has been passed which in turn is generating a growing body of case law. Further legislation is thought likely. Here we can only attempt a brief summary of the more important aspects of this field as it affects the individual health visitor. It will help to alert you to your rights and duties and will provide a guide if a problem arises. In practice the number of cases where a health visitor goes to an Industrial Tribunal is minimal. But if you are unlucky enough to have a problem, you should consult your professional association or a solicitor at once. The law imposes strict time limits within which an action must be begun in the courts or before an industrial tribunal, and an action begun outside those limits can generally be struck out (though there are exceptions), probably leaving you with no remedy. The Department of Employment publishes a series of booklets[2] which explain the main provisions of the Employment Acts in simple and succinct language. These are available from Jobcentres, Employment Offices and Unemployment Benefit Offices and sometimes from Citizens' Advice Bureaux and public libraries. A booklet normally comes out for each new Act. Finally remember that the relationship

2. Department of Employment, Employment Legislation Series, 1–15.

27

between employer and employee (and in your case your superiors also) is primarily one between people. If you can maintain good and amicable relations, many problems can be avoided because they never arise.

Your employer will give you a written statement of the main terms and conditions of your contract within thirteen weeks of your starting work, and of any changes to it within a month.[3,4] This statement will include *inter alia* your name and your employers', the title of your job, the date of commencing employment, terms relating to pay, hours of work, holiday leave and pay, illness, sick pay, pension, length of notice by either side to terminate, and an additional note on disciplinary and grievance procedures. The contract itself may be oral or implied by conduct (i.e. starting work), and is enforceable whether in writing or not. Although the 1978 Act requires a written statement of its main terms and gives one the right of recourse to an industrial tribunal in default, this does not apply to the NHS.[5]

You receive as well the right to a minimum period of notice of dismissal which applies unless either your contract provides for a longer period, or, generally, it is for a fixed term. The relevant period of notice is at least one week after four weeks' or more continuous employment,[6] at least two weeks after two years' or more continuous employment, and an additional week for each complete year of continuous employment up to a maximum of twelve weeks.[7] Generally you are entitled to be paid for this period of notice, but if you receive insufficient notice and do not accept payment in lieu, you can sue your employers for damages for breach of contract (i.e. the salary you would have earned). But the Act preserves the employers' common law right of summary dismissal for misconduct.

After four weeks' continuous employment you must give your employers at least one week's notice, but this does not increase with longer service. Your contract, though, may provide for a longer period, in which case you must honour it. If not, the above rule will apply. If you give insufficient notice or leave before the end of a fixed term, your employers can sue you for any actual loss and damage suffered, but they can never obtain a court order compelling you to work for them, and it is unlikely they would be able to obtain an injunction preventing you obtaining other employment.

Special regulations apply to National Health Service employees.[8] These require all employing authorities to implement agreements reached by all the Whitley Councils and confirmed by the Secretary of State. The Nurses and Midwives Whitley Council covers health visitors. Some Whitley Council

---

3. See further Department of Employment, booklet 1, plus the special booklet on the Contracts of Employment Act 1972 (now part of the 1978 Act).
4. This does not apply at all if one normally works less than eight hours a week, and only after five years if one normally works less than sixteen hours a week.
5. This jurisdiction lasts throughout the employment but, generally, only for three months on termination.
6. See further Department of Employment, booklet 11.
7. If the Act applies, it guarantees minimum pay during notice (or pay in lieu of notice): DoE, booklet 14.
8. National Health Service (Remuneration and Conditions of Service) Regulations 1974 (S.I. 1974 No. 296).

agreements give the employee more generous rights than the relevant Acts. So again the precise terms of your contract are crucial.

Neither side may waive their rights under the Whitley Council Agreement.

b. Your employers' duties: During your employment your employers owe you certain duties. The most important are:

(a) to pay your salary (less permitted deductions) in cash, or by cheque, postal order or money order – unless you leave without proper notice or are summarily dismissed for good cause.[9]

(b) to provide a safe place and system of work (see p 33).

(c) to provide proper and suitable equipment and keep it in a safe condition.

(d) to reimburse expenses arising directly out of your employment, unless arising from your default.

(e) to select reasonably fit and competent fellow employees.

(f) to ensure so far as reasonably practicable the health, safety and welfare at work of all their employees.

(g) not to dismiss you unfairly and after 26 weeks to give you written reasons for dismissal on request.

(h) not to discriminate against you on grounds of race or sex (including marital status).[10]

(i) to allow you reasonable time off for public duties,[11] or duties as a trade union official.

(j) not to penalise you in any way for any trade union activities in which you are involved.

(k) to observe certain special duties owed to women.

If your employers break any of (a) to (e), you can bring a case against them through the courts, or, in the case of (g) to (k) before an industrial tribunal.[12]

Unfair dismissal (g) includes where you are forced to resign through a serious breach of contract by your employers, and if you are a woman, preventing you returning to work after having a baby. These are examples of constructive dismissal.

If you are wrongfully dismissed you can sue your employers in court for the amount you would have earned, as damages, less income tax on the first £25,000 unemployment benefit and any earnings from alternative employment. If you are unfairly dismissed, you can seek an order for compensation or for reinstatement or re-engagement[12] from an industrial tribunal, but you must initiate proceedings within three months of ceasing employment, unless

---

9. You also have the right to an itemised pay statement: DoE booklet 8; and to guarantee payments: DoE, booklet 9.

10. There is an exception for hospitals discriminating on grounds of sex: S.7 of the Sex Discrimination Act 1975.

11. See Department of Employment, booklet 12.

12. Damages are normally the only remedy available from a court. You cannot obtain a court order compelling your employer to employ you. Damages are not available on summary dismissal for misconduct.

you can show that it was not reasonably practicable to do so.[13] Damages for breach of contract are a common law remedy and have always been available to an employee. The concept of unfair dismissal was introduced by the Industrial Relations Act 1971, which was replaced by the Trade Union and Labour Relations Act 1974 and is now part of the 1978 Act. It rests on the premise that employees have something akin to a right of property in their jobs and should not be deprived of them without due cause.

In either case you must mitigate your loss by trying to find another job. If you do not try, your damages or compensation may be reduced accordingly.

Generally, if you have been continuously employed by your employers (i.e. the actual health authority employing you) for fifty-two weeks or more for at least sixteen hours a week (or for five years or more for at least eight hours a week),[14] your dismissal will be presumed to be unfair unless your employers prove firstly that the reason, or principal reason, was either

(a) your capability or qualifications for the work you were employed to do (e.g. if you were struck off after disciplinary proceedings); or

(b) your conduct; or

(c) redundancy, provided you were fairly selected;[15] or

(d) that your continued employment would contravene a statutory requirement (e.g. a safety requirement);[16] or

(e) your refusal to join a trade union where there is a closed shop;[17] or

(f) dismissal in relation to a strike or a lock-out, provided certain conditions are satisfied (e.g. all participating employees are treated alike); or

(g) some other substantial reason.

Secondly, it depends whether in the circumstances (including the size and adminstrative resources of their undertaking) your employers acted reasonably in treating the chosen reason as sufficient ground for dismissal.[18] Generally you have the right to be heard before being dismissed, and where appropriate, warned.

Health visitors have an extra remedy on dismissal. Under the General Whitley Council agreement they, like all National Health Service employees, can appeal to a committee of the employing authority. This appeal should always precede a hearing by an industrial tribunal, though not necessarily notice of appeal to the tribunal, but this right begins on appointment.

When an employee becomes pregnant, she may acquire four special

13. Between dismissal and presenting a claim to an industrial tribunal you may ask the Advisory Conciliation and Arbitration Service ACAS to conciliate. If so, an officer must seek agreement between you and your employers on compensation, reinstatement or re-engagement. The addresses of the Regional Directors of ACAS (to whom you should apply) are available from the Department of Employment. After a claim is presented to them, ACAS always seeks conciliation.
14. See further Department of Employment, booklet 13; there are certain exceptions, where a lower limit (on certain medical grounds), or even no limit, applies (e.g. dismissal for trade union membership or activities, or where discrimination is alleged).
15. But you are entitled to reasonable time off, with pay, for job hunting or to arrange training.
16. This would not apply to a health visitor.
17. Though all health visitors must be qualified, membership of the Health Visitors' Association is voluntary and thus this would not apply to a health visitor.
18. The ACAS Code of Practice can be important here.

rights:[19] (a) reasonable time off, with pay, for antenatal care; (b) to claim unfair dismissal if she is dismissed because of pregnancy or for a reason relating to pregnancy; (c) maternity pay; (d) to return to work with her employers afterwards. If she is denied one or more of these rights, she can complain to an industrial tribunal. But she must normally do so within three months. The 1978 Act does not give her the right to maternity leave as such or to her salary during such leave. But if (a) she has been continuously employed by her employers for at least two years for sixteen hours or more a week (or five years for eight hours or more a week) by the start of the eleventh week before her expected week of confinement, and (b) she continues that employment up to that date, and (c) she gives her employers notice in writing at least twenty-one days beforehand (or, if this is not reasonably practicable, as soon afterwards as it is so), and (d) she gives, if requested, a doctor's or midwife's certificate, then she has firstly the right to maternity pay (i.e. 90 per cent of her pay, minus the flat-rate national insurance maternity allowance, for six weeks) and secondly the right to return to her job any time up to twenty-nine weeks[20] after the week of her baby's birth. If her employers ask her in writing to confirm her intention to return (which may not be done before forty-nine days from the start either of her expected week of confinement or of the actual confinement) she must reply in writing within fourteen days, or, if this is not reasonably practicable, as soon afterwards as it is so. She must also notify her employers in writing of her proposed date of return at least twenty-one days beforehand. The right to return does not apply if her employers can show that reinstatement is not reasonably practicable, and suitable alternative employment has been offered and either accepted or unreasonably refused. If, however, her job has ceased to exist through redundancy she must be offered any suitable alternative job which is available. These are her statutory rights, but the relevant General Whitley Council agreement provides additional rights.

The Health Visitor is Injured

What happens if you have the misfortune to be injured on duty? As soon as possible after the injury[21] you should consider your legal position. Firstly, can you sue for damages, and if so whom? Secondly, are you entitled to any social security benefit?

a. Damages: If you wish to sue for damages you should consult your professional association first, then if necessary a solicitor, or your Legal Officer.[22] Here we can only attempt a brief summary of the claims you are most likely to have and against whom. This will help you to spot a potential claim and give you a guide as to what you can claim for, but it is not exhaustive, so you will still need legal advice.

To recover damages of any sort, you must first show that you have suffered

---

19. See further Department of Employment, booklet 4.
20. In certain circumstances she may claim an extra four weeks in the case of illness.
21. Under the Limitation Act 1980 actions for personal injuries must generally be brought within three years, though there are exceptions.
22. If you are contemplating suing your employers, it would of course be inappropriate to consult your Legal Officer.

some loss or damage. There are two sorts of damage at law, general and special.

General damages include such things as an amount to cover the pain and suffering your injuries have caused and will cause you, and the amount appropriate for those injuries. It is, of course, difficult to quantify such things in money, but over the years the courts have evolved approximate set figures for almost every injury. Of late these figures have been increased to allow for inflation, and this is likely to continue as long as inflation. General damages also cover expected future loss, e.g. loss of expectation of life,[23] future loss of earnings and future expenses. The likelihood of future inflation is ignored and future earnings and expenses are only awarded to cover a set number of years fixed by the court, the usual maximum being twenty.

Special damages cover each item of financial loss you have actually suffered, e.g. loss of earnings to date, damage to clothing and other property, medical treatment (even if as a private patient) and fares to and from hospital. However, you must deduct from any damages for loss of earnings income tax, unemployment benefit, supplementary benefit, and half any sickness or industrial injury benefit.[24] This is because damages are to compensate you for the loss you have actually suffered and not to punish the person causing the damage or to afford you a windfall. However, you can claim interest on certain parts of your award.

You must ensure that you tell your legal adviser of each item of financial loss that you have suffered so that it can be claimed. But in each case you must show that the loss has resulted directly from the wrongful act of the person you are suing. Loss which is not caused at all by the wrongful act cannot be recovered. Nor can loss which the law regards as too remote (i.e. not resulting sufficiently directly from the wrongful act). Also if you have consented or in some way contributed to the loss you have suffered, your damages will be reduced accordingly, possibly, if appropriate, to nothing.

For example, suppose you are involved in a road accident which was partly your fault and partly the other driver's. Your damages will be reduced by the percentage which the court finds that you were to blame.[25]

Suppose you are applying for a new post as a health visitor. You miss the interview, and thus lose the job, because you are delayed in a traffic jam caused by an accident. You cannot sue the person responsible for the accident, because your loss is too remote.

In a recent case the manager of a butcher's shop was injured at work. He was then found to be suffering from myelopathy which would soon have proved totally disabling. The Court of Appeal held the myelopathy should be taken into account and his damages reduced accordingly.

---

23. This receives a set and modest amount, currently (1982) about £1,000.
24. You do not have to deduct other insurance payments, or disablement pension, but you may have to deduct salary paid by your employers during illness, particularly if they are legally bound to pay (the courts have not finally decided this yet).
25. Your damages will also, generally, be reduced if you do not wear a seat belt, or travel in a car knowing the driver to be under the influence of drink, or ride a motor-cycle without wearing a crash helmet.

Damages are not recoverable for mere sorrow or grief, but they are for nervous shock or a psychiatric illness caused, for example, by the sight of an accident, at any rate one to a close relative.

Once you have received your damages, you cannot sue for more, even if your injuries prove more serious than was at first thought or because inflation diminishes their value. To hedge against inflation, you must invest your money prudently and if necessary take professional investment advice, and you must mitigate your loss if you can.

You must show also that a wrongful act has been committed. Normally for a health visitor on duty this will mean showing either negligence by someone at common law, or that someone is in breach of a statutory duty, or that an occupier of premises is liable under the Occupiers' Liability Act 1957.[26]

To establish negligence by someone at common law you must show that they have broken a common law duty of care which they owed to you and have been negligent. This can apply to a wide (though not unlimited) variety of situations. For example, if you are injured in a road accident through the negligent driving of someone else[27] or if you slip over a yoghurt spilled on a patient's kitchen floor and break your wrist.[28]

Your employers owe you the normal common law duty of care, but also a special common law duty to provide a safe system and place of work. This duty covers personal injuries to you, but not normally loss resulting from theft of your property, nor damage suffered outside your employment, e.g. on your way to work.

Your employers are liable for their negligence, but they are not an insurer of your safety, and you must bear the risks which necessarily accompany your work. For example, it is unlikely that you could sucessfully sue your employers for an illness contracted from a client.

Suing for breach of statutory duty will normally involve suing your employers, or (if the accident happened in a school) the Local Education Authority. Here you must show that whoever you are suing was under a statutory duty to do something which they failed to execute. You must also show that the breach in question gives rise to civil liability for damages. For example the Health and Safety at Work etc. Act 1974 imposes a general statutory duty on both employers and employees, but expressly creates no civil liability. Claims under this head can often be brought in common law negligence as well.

Under the Occupiers' Liability Act 1957 the occupier of premises owes a duty to all lawful visitors to take all reasonable care to ensure their reasonable safety while on the premises. Normally a health visitor will be a lawful visitor even when visiting a new family unexpected and uninvited. But you must still be careful, particularly if you are warned of dangers (verbally or in writing –

---

26. Certain special considerations apply where an accident is fatal, but generally, if you had a claim your executors or administrators will have one.
27. If you are a passenger, you sue the driver whose fault the accident was, or if this is doubtful both drivers.
28. Remember that you will be liable if you negligently damage a patient or client's property when visiting their home.

e.g. "Beware of the Dog"), because the warning may extinguish your right to damages. And once you have been asked to leave, you must normally do so forthwith, because otherwise you become a trespasser, and the occupier is only liable where the law considers that as a matter of common humanity they should be. This doctrine tends to be applied to children playing on unfenced railway lines and such like rather than to health visitors. Finally claims under this head can again usually be brought in common law negligence as well.

Thirdly, whom do you sue? You can always sue the person causing the damage, but there is little point in suing someone who cannot pay, which is often the case with the offending party. If however they are insured, the insurance company will generally pay any damages. Under the Road Traffic Act 1972 it is a criminal offence to drive a car without being insured against third party liability, and against passenger liability. Some people break the law, but if you are injured by an uninsured driver you may be able to sue the Motor Insurers' Bureau.

Many house insurance policies nowadays cover public liability (i.e. occupiers' liability to visitors). But if you are injured in a patient or client's home, it would be prudent to check before suing whether your claim will be covered by insurance (unless, of course, the family are wealthy folk well able to pay any damages themselves). Also if the property is rented, the landlord may sometimes be liable.

If the person causing the damage is an employee who committed the wrongful act in the course of that employee's employment, then the employer is usually liable simply through being the employer. This would very often apply if, for example, you were injured by the negligence of the driver of a commercial vehicle, or of builders working at a patient or client's home. In such cases you normally sue both the person causing the damage and the employer.

b. Social Security: Each month your employers make a PAYE payment to the Collector of Taxes. This includes income tax previously deducted from your salary plus your employee's contribution to Class 1 national insurance similarly deducted, and their employers' Class 1 contribution. You have to pay Class 1 contributions as long as you are employed and are aged 18 and under 60 for women or 65 for men. In return certain social security benefits arise if you become ill, are injured or killed or become unemployed, and you will receive your state pension when you retire.[29] Your pension is payable at 60 for women and 65 for men, but if you earn over a specified limit your pension will be reduced accordingly. Once women reach 65 and men reach 70, their pensions are payable irrespective of any earnings. Pensions may also be reduced if there have been insufficient contributions. The rates of contributions are fixed in advance for each year in the Budget.

Social security is a complicated area of the law, and there are many different benefits for those who fall within the above-mentioned categories. The most

---

29. In addition there are social security benefits for children, expectant mothers, the handicapped and disabled, widows, those with very low incomes and those injured in the war or H.M. Forces.

important one for the health visitor is Industrial Injury Benefit, which is payable to all employees injured at work (including fatally) without proof of negligence by anyone, if they are off work for a period or their earning capacity is lost or reduced. Pain and suffering receive no compensation. If you have a problem, or wish to claim a benefit, you should consult your local social security office (or indeed any social security office). They will be pleased to advise you and issue leaflets explaining in simple language each benefit, class of contribution and so on.[30] If you still have a problem, your professional association may be able to help. Otherwise you can consult a solicitor.

Finally, as a National Health Service employee, if you are injured on duty (which does not include travelling from home to normal duty) or contract a disease through exposure to it by the nature of your work, you can claim under the Service's Injury Benefit Scheme.[31] Also if your injury resulted from a crime, you may be able to claim compensation from the Criminal Injuries Compensation Board.

THE LEGAL DUTIES OF THE HEALTH VISITOR

Rights and duties are correlatives. Having discussed the main rights of the health visitor, we must now look at the duties.

The Health Visitor – an Employee

You owe your employers certain duties, both during and after your employment. The most important are:

(a) to carry out their lawful instructions.

(b) to render them faithful service.

(c) not to be absent from work without good cause.

(d) not to disclose confidential information obtained in the course of your employment.[32]

(e) to perform your duties with reasonable care (see below).

(f) to take reasonable care for the health and safety of others and to co-operate with your employer in this.

You can be dismissed if you break duties (a), (b), (c) or (e) (provided the dismissal is not wrongful or unfair) or you may have to compensate your employers for actual loss or damage suffered.

Professional Negligence

The fear of being sued for professional negligence worries many professional people. Actions for medical negligence really began after the last war with the inception of the National Health Service and legal aid. Today they cannot be ignored.

---

30. This advice also holds good if a patient or client has a social security problem.
31. For details see S.27 of the Members' Guide to the National Health Service Superannuation Scheme; and document A.W. 155 by the DHSS Superannuation Division.
32. This duty continues after the termination of your employment, and can probably be enforced by an injunction.

How can you protect yourself? From your nursing training you will know that there is no foolproof way of ensuring that you never make a mistake. But you can be careful.

So, what is professional negligence? As a health visitor you owe the common law duty of care to each of your patients and clients. If you break that duty by giving negligent advice or negligent treatment you are generally liable for any damage which results.

What constitutes negligent advice or treatment? The law requires a high standard of the medical and nursing professions because, like all professional people, they profess a special skill. But it does not require perfection. The test is, did you show "the standard of the ordinary skilled man exercising and professing to have that special skill"?[33] This means that if you advise or do what an ordinarily competent health visitor would not advise or do, you are likely to be liable in negligence, so you must keep your knowledge and skill up to date. You are not liable merely because you have not read every article in the medical and nursing press, and this special standard only applies to any medical and nursing advice which you give.[34] So if you helped a client with their domestic chores it is thought that you would only be expected to show the skill of an ordinary housewife, and further, that if you had to undertake medical work well outside the normal run of health visiting, for example in an emergency, you would only be expected to show the skill of an ordinarily competent health visitor and not that, say, of a surgeon.[35]

You are only liable for a mere error of judgement if it is a mistake which no ordinarily competent health visitor would have made. As Lord Denning M.R. said "If they [i.e. medical men] are to be found liable [for negligence] whenever they do not effect a cure, or whenever anything untoward happens, it would do a great disservice to the profession itself."[36]

Thus if there are two schools of medical thought, you are not negligent if you follow one of them, provided it is "accepted as proper by a responsible body of medical men skilled in that particular art" and you are not liable "merely because there is a body of opinion who would take the contrary view".[37] But you cannot allow yourself the luxury of "blind spots" or "hobby-horses" and your personal opinion is only sufficient if it is based on reasonable grounds (i.e. a responsible body of medical opinion). Perhaps the most sensible advice is, if medical opinion is divided, explain both schools of thought to the patient or client and let them make up their own mind. Express your own opinion if necessary (after all some patients and clients decline to make up their own minds), but make it clear what you are doing.

33. Bolam v. Friern Management Committee [1957] 1 W.L.R. 582, 586 *(per* McNair J.). Approved by House of Lords in the case of Whitehouse v. Jordan [1981] 1 W.L.R. 246, 258 A–D *per* Lord Edmund-Davies.
34. Stokes v. Guest Keen & Nettlefold (Bolts & Nuts) Ltd. [1968] 1 W.L.R. 1776, 1783 F–4G where Swanwick J. held that this standard applied to the medical aspects of advice given by a factory doctor but not to the economic and administrative aspects.
35. See Phillips v. William Whiteley Ltd. [1938] 1 A.E.R. 566, 568H–569E where it was held that a jeweller was not expected to show the same skill as a surgeon at earpiercing.
36. Whitehouse v. Jordan [1981] 1 W.L.R. p 246, 263 C–D.
37. Bolam v. Friern Hospital Management Committee at p 587.

Inexperience is no defence, though it may be very relevant on the question of contribution. In one case a patient died because the anaesthetist, who had only five months' experience, administered twice the required dose of anaesthetic. The Court of Appeal held that the hospital should pay 80 per cent of the damages, the anaesthetist 20 per cent.[38]

Finally, even if you are negligent, any claim against you will fail if you can show that your negligence did not cause the damage. For instance, three night-watchmen went to casualty complaining of three hours vomiting and abdominal pains. The duty medical officer told the nurse over the telephone to send them home. They went, and one died of arsenical poisoning. The claim failed because, though the officer was negligent in not seeing and admitting them, the man might have died even had he been admitted.[39]

Negligence is a question of fact in each case, and the court is the judge, not your peers. But there are no varying degrees of negligence. Either the duty of care is broken or it is not. As we said earlier a higher standard is expected of professional people exercising their skill, but that is another matter. If there is a dispute as to the facts, it is the trial judge who must decide whose version is to be preferred. For further cases see Appendix II section c.

Health visitors face special problems here because of the multi-disciplinary nature of their work. What is their job? This is a difficult problem, but if this question arose in court the views of the Health Visitors' Association expressed in *Health Visiting in the '80s* would be likely to carry weight as representing the views of "a responsible body of medical men skilled in that particular art".

There are two things you can do to protect yourself against claims. Firstly, take care to avoid being negligent; and secondly, take out professional indemnity insurance.

There is no foolproof system. This is firstly because to be human is to make mistakes, and secondly because each case is judged on its own facts and merits rather than by strict legal rules. However, the following further tips should prove helpful:

(a) always ensure that your advice is as accurate as possible. Never do or advise what you know is wrong. There is no excuse if you do. Do not guarantee the efficacy of any treatment or course of action you recommend. The law does not require such a guarantee and it may prove unwarranted.

(b) always be willing to take a little extra trouble in whatever you do (whether it be checking the accuracy of your advice, or passing on information to your GP or local social services department). Act when you find something wrong (if action is needed). Do not just note. This is a counsel of perfection, but remember the time you slip up may be the time disaster strikes, and such counsels are an anchor-rope to stop you slipping too far.

(c) always try to maintain good relations with your client. A breakdown in these precedes many allegations of professional negligence.

38. Jones v. Manchester Corporation [1952] 2 Q.B. 852.
39. Barnett v. Chelsea and Kensington Hospital Management Committee [1969] 1 Q.B. 428.

(d) except in an emergency, do not go outside your own sphere of competence.

(e) keep notes and records which are adequate, legible and signed. This is your best defence against a negligence action based on inaccurate facts. And remember that when the facts are disputed a judge must decide.

(f) keep all correspondence that you receive, and keep copies of all letters you send.

(g) never admit liability, except on legal advice.

(h) do not disclose that you are insured. Knowing that you are insured encourages a certain type of patient to sue.

Professional indemnity insurance is desirable for all practising health visitors, and most relevant professional associations provide it with their subscription, so you should make inquiries of them. If you prefer not to belong to a professional association, you can obtain indemnity policies from insurance companies, but in that case you should seek legal advice to make sure that you are getting the protection you require.

In practice, however, it is unlikely that you will need to have recourse to your policy, because your employing authority is vicariously liable for any negligence you commit in the course of your employment. In practice also it is normally they, and not you, who are sued and, though they can claim an indemnity from you, they do not. If, on the other hand, you use your professional skills in your spare time (e.g. to help a friend) and are negligent, your employers will almost certainly not be liable, although they might be liable if you were acting in an emergency (e.g. "first on the scene" after an accident).

Lastly, three words of encouragement. Advising is less hazardous than treating. So the health visitor is much less at risk than other members of the nursing and medical professions. Indeed the number of actions against health visitors to date has been minimal. As a health visitor you have a job to do, so be careful, but do not allow the fear of a negligence action stop you doing that job. Finally, it may be that one day negligence actions will be replaced by a central fund on which those who suffer loss can claim irrespective of whether the medical advice or treatment they received was negligent or not.

Treating Patients and Trespass To Person

Assault is where the defendant causes the plaintiff reasonable fear that a physical attack on them is about to follow. The least touching in anger is "battery", as is any intentional application of force to another. Any physical contact with the plaintiff's body is sufficient to amount to "force". In common parlance "assault" covers both assault and battery, but at law they are separate terms with distinct meanings. An example may make this clearer. Throwing a bucket of water at someone is assault (because they fear a soaking), but wetting them with it is battery. Assault and battery are criminal offences as well as civil wrongs.

How does this affect the health visitor? The definition of battery is sufficiently wide to cover medical treatment. Thus anyone who treats a patient and does it without their consent may be sued for battery. Attempted treatment would make them liable for assault or battery as appropriate. In both cases a prosecution could follow.[40] A health visitor's primary function is to advise, and normally speech cannot constitute assault or battery, though it can give rise to a negligence action. But most health visitors administer some treatment from time to time (e.g. changing a dressing).

Consent is a complete defence.[41] So always ensure you have the patient's consent before treating them. Merely knowing that treatment is taking place is not enough, but provided the patient clearly indicates consent, you should be alright.[42] The consent must be real and the patient must understand in broad terms the nature of the treatment proposed. This was established in a case which concerned two intrathecal injections of phenol solution by an analgesia specialist, to create a nerve block to alleviate chronic pain after a right herniorrhaphy operation – the treatment proving unsuccessful.[43] This does not mean that you must explain every detail of any proposed treatment, but it does mean, for example, that consent to a tonsilectomy would not constitute consent to a circumcision performed by mistake, or that consent to excise a verruca would constitute consent to treat an ingrowing toe-nail. But consent to treat a verruca pedis would no doubt constitute consent to treat a mosaic verruca – particularly if you just said you were treating a verruca.

There is an exception to these rules in the case of necessity, for example where someone is unconscious. Here treatment may be administered without consent, provided what is done is reasonably necessary. However, it is generally accepted that except in an emergency the consent of the next-of-kin is needed even here.

A second sort of trespass to person is False Imprisonment, which is bodily restraint of a person without lawful authority. This will not normally concern the health visitor, but you must not normally detain your clients or patients against their will. Similarly they may not detain you against your will. But in either case the restraint must be total to be false imprisonment, though the victim need not know of the restraint.

Special considerations apply to children. Once they are 16 they may consent to lawful surgical, medical or dental treatment, and the consent of the parent or guardian is not needed.[44] Under that age you must always have the parent or guardian's permission. However, provided you have that, it is generally accepted that you may carry out treatment even though the child, as often

---

40. Any health visitor who has the misfortune to be the victim of an assault or battery can sue, and, if desired, prosecute. You may also use "reasonable force" to defend yourself.
41. Consent, however, cannot authorise an unlawful act: e.g. a patient's consent to euthanasia or an unlawful abortion would not prevent the doctor's prosecution.
42. cf. Bennett v. Tugwell [1971] 2 W.L.R. 847, 852A where Ackner J. said that the test is objective, i.e. if one could reasonably believe consent was given, it does not matter if the patient did not intend to consent.
43. Chatterton v. Gerson [1980] 3 W.L.R. 1003 (Bristow J.) at p 1012 D–13 E.
44. S.8 of the Family Law Reform Act 1969.

happens, protests vigorously.[45] If the child is over 16 the law is unclear, but it is thought on balance that the parent or guardian's consent is not sufficient, except where the child is unconscious.

a. Pupils at school: Children at maintained schools come under the Schools Health Service and further special considerations apply to them, and will concern the health visitor who is a School Nurse.

Under the National Health Service Act 1977 the Secretary of State must provide medical and dental inspection and treatment at appropriate intervals for pupils at schools maintained by local education authorities. By Statutory Instrument, the Regional Health Authority must exercise these functions on behalf of the Secretary of State. Under the Education Act 1944, the local education authority must encourage and assist pupils to use these services, unless a parent gives notice of objection.

The Secretary of State and the local education authority are given certain statutory powers to inspect and treat pupils.

For the state system of education the Secretary of State (i.e. for Education and Science in England, and for Wales in Wales) has power under Section 69 (2) of the 1944 Act to require a pupil to be examined by a doctor appointed for the purpose. Written notice must be served on the pupil's parent (or, at a county college, the pupil). There is a fine for non-compliance.

Under Section 54 of the 1944 Act a local education authority can authorise in writing one of their medical officers to examine the person and clothing (including footwear) of pupils at their maintained schools whenever they consider this necessary in the interests of cleanliness. They may also have a pupil at a county college examined where that pupil's person or clothing are reasonably suspected of being infested with vermin or in a foul condition. If vermin or a foul condition are found the pupil's parent (or at a county college the pupil) may be ordered to cleanse that pupil's person or clothing.

If the cleansing is not carried out, the medical officer may order it to be done by the local education authority. This order is sufficient to authorise any officer of the authority to have the person and clothing of the pupil named in it cleansed in accordance with that authority's arrangements and to take and detain that pupil at the premises provided under those arrangements.[46] But a girl may only be cleansed by a doctor or a woman authorised by the authority. Health visitors should be clear that without such an order they have no power to compel treatment. They can only try to persuade either the parent or guardian (or the pupil if over 16) to allow treatment or their superiors to procure an order. Even with an order, they must not exceed the powers it gives. If they do, they are liable.

A medical officer may order a pupil to be excluded from school pending cleansing, where necessary in the interests of that pupil or of other pupils.

In certain circumstances local education authorities have power to provide clothing for pupils.

---

45. Probably the same applies to persons of unsound mind.
46. S.54 (5) of the 1944 Act.

40

b. Mental patients: Under the Mental Health Act 1959 there is power to admit and detain a patient compulsorily in hospital or to place a patient under compulsory guardianship of the local social services authority or someone approved by them. The authority must visit patients subject to guardianship. The grounds are that the patient is suffering from mental disorder warranting admission or guardianship and is a danger to others or in personal danger. An application for admission is sufficient authority for the applicant, or anyone the applicant authorises, to take the patient to hospital and for the patient's detention there. An application for guardianship gives the guardian the powers of a father over a child under 14. Criminal courts can order an offender to be treated for mental disorder (a "hospital order") or to be placed in guardianship (a "guardianship order"). The Crown Court can make a restriction on discharge. A hospital order is sufficient authority for whoever the court directs to take the patient to hospital and for the patient's detention there.

Motor Cars

One problem which often worries health visitors is their position at law if they are involved in a road accident. The basic rule is that if you are involved in an accident which is your fault you are liable to all those injured. If it was the other driver's fault, the other driver is liable.

If the accident was partly your fault and partly that of the other driver, the court can apportion between the drivers the damages it awards to a passenger in either car, a pedestrian or the like under the Civil Liability (Contribution) Act 1978. In this situation the passenger or pedestrian would normally sue all the drivers involved, and this is so also where it is unclear who is to blame. But the damages payable by you to the other driver will be reduced by the amount the court finds the other driver to blame, and the same applies to any damages payable to you. This is based on the principle of contributory negligence touched on before.

Let us now assume the accident was your fault. Who pays the damages? As the person who caused it you are always liable and you will normally be sued. However, the damages may well be paid either by your employers or by your insurance company. If at the time of the accident you were driving in the course of your employment your employers are liable. Whether this applies or not depends entirely on the facts of the case. But normally, if you are driving on duty, your employers will be liable. This is so, even if, for example, you make a brief detour to have some lunch. But it probably does not apply if, for example, you drive many miles into the country to have a picnic, even though you are on duty at the time. It certainly does not apply if you are driving either your own car or a Crown car with your employers' permission for, say, a social engagement when off duty, or if you are on your way to or from work. But the dividing line depends on the facts of the case, and is not always clear cut.

Your employers are liable for everything expressly or impliedly authorised in the course of your employment and for all the damage thereby caused, whether to another driver, or to a pedestrian, or to a patient or fellow

41

employee in your car.[47] This is so, whether you are driving your own car or a Crown car, because your negligent driving caused the accident.[48]

Your employers are also liable sometimes if you do something which is not authorised or even something expressly forbidden. This problem will arise in practice if, for example, your employers forbid you to give lifts. Again, the dividing line is not clear cut but depends on the facts of each case. But it is likely that your employers are probably not liable for injuries even to patients and fellow employees who are unauthorised passengers and certainly not for injuries to casual passengers (e.g. hitch-hikers and friends). However, there may be special circumstances which make your employers liable, for example if the lift was part of your work, like taking a student with you for training purposes, or if there was an emergency, e.g. you were rushing a failed suicide or a difficult birth to hospital.

Again it makes no difference whose car you are driving. But if you are forbidden by your employers to carry passengers, it is strongly recommended that you take out insurance cover. Also if you are unlucky enough to be involved in an accident you should take legal advice at once and never under any circumstances admit liability except on legal advice. Do not even apologise after the accident. If the accident is not your fault you should take the names and addresses of any witnesses. Independent witnesses will carry a good deal of weight in both criminal and civil proceedings, but they are apt to disappear after an accident. Following an accident you must (a) stop, and (b) if requested by anyone having reasonable cause (e.g. the other driver), give your name, address and particulars of the car. Where personal injury to another person occurs you must also give insurance details. If no such information is requested at the time of the accident the driver(s) must report to the police within 24 hours and a certificate of insurance must be produced to them within five days of the accident. (For further information see Section 25 of the Road Traffic Act 1972). You must also report injuries to animals, unless carried in your own car or trailer, and this includes dogs, cattle and horses, but not cats and birds.

Finally, even if your employer is liable, the court may order you to contribute the proportion of the damages it finds just and equitable in view of your degree of responsibility, which may amount to your paying all the damages.[49]

Let us now assume you are injured in the accident. If you are a passenger and the accident is the fault of your fellow employee, as the driver, then your employers are liable to you for their employee's negligence and can be sued

---

47. It is not clear if your employers are liable to a casual passenger, e.g. a friend or a hitch-hiker, who is unconnected with your work; but your employers may well not be liable.

48. Different considerations may apply if a fault in your car caused the accident.

49. Civil Liability (Contribution) Act 1978. For professional negligence it seems your employers could also recover any damages from you under an implied indemnity in your contract: Lister v. Romford Ice and Cold Storage Co. Ltd. [1957] A.C. 555, where a lorry driver took his father as a mate; the father was injured through his son's negligence. The House of Lords held the son must pay the damages. But this does not necessarily apply if you have a road accident. Harvey v. R. G. O'Dell Ltd. [1958] 2 Q.B. 78, where the driver causing the accident was employed as a storekeeper, not a driver, and McNair J. held that there was no implied indemnity.

except where the lift was unauthorised. If it is the other driver's fault, you can sue that driver. The same applies if you are the driver and it is the other driver's fault. But if you are the driver and the accident is your fault, you cannot sue anyone. However, you may become entitled to industrial injury benefit, provided you are driving on duty and you should be covered by your own insurance. In any event, if you are injured you should take legal advice as soon as possible if there is any question of your bringing a claim.

The best financial protection against the consequences of road accidents is insurance, and Part VI of the Road Traffic Act 1972 requires all motor car owners to have third party insurance, and passenger cover is now also required. Failure to comply is a criminal offence. Most motorists, however, consider that, unless there are special circumstances, comprehensive insurance is necessary, and it is therefore recommended that health visitors should have some sort of comprehensive cover.

The extent of your insurance cover depends on the contract between you and the insurance company. So if you already have cover, you should read the terms of your policy carefully, and if you are taking out a new policy, you should read the terms of the prospective policy carefully and check that they meet your requirements. If necessary, you should talk the matter over with your insurance company or broker. But remember that when taking out or renewing insurance cover you must show the utmost good faith, and disclose all matters which might be in any way material to whether the insurance company will accept the risk, especially any convictions for road traffic offences. If you do not, the company may be able to void the policy and leave you without cover. Usually you must notify them immediately of any expected claims and your rights to pursue or defend a claim will often be taken over by the company.

If you drive your own car, you must have third party cover and passenger cover. You should consider insurance *inter alia* to cover (a) yourself, (b) your equipment and/or belongings, (c) your vehicle. By special arrangement the principal insurance companies have agreed to indemnify employing authorities against vicarious liability on third party claims (but excluding claims by a passenger who is a fellow employee) under your policy.[50] But you must have the written acceptance of your insurance company of the fact that you use your car for work. If you are not insured with one of these companies[51] you must obtain a suitable endorsement on your policy. In return for this indemnity you receive a mileage allowance.

Part VI of the Road Traffic Act 1972 does not apply to Health Authorities,[52] so their cars are uninsured. If you are driving one you should consider cover *inter alia* for yourself, your equipment and/or belongings, as they will not otherwise be covered at all, and, if there is any question of your employer not being liable, third party and passengers. This is particularly important as the

50. See circular R.B.H. (50) 122, as amended by H.M. (54) 26.
51. They are listed in the appendix to R.B.H. (50) 122.
52. S.144 (2) (f) of the 1972 Act as added by National Health Service (Vehicles) Order 1974 (S.I. 1974 No. 168), Art 4.

NHS are not usually willing to help you pursue a claim for damages if you are injured when driving a Crown car.

Undue Influence

Suppose a patient or client offers you a gift, a small token of appreciation. To refuse may give offence. If your employing authority has rules about this, you should know and observe them. The courts have set aside gifts where the client has been subjected to 'undue influence' which means where the gift was not made entirely of the client's own free will. It is probably better to avoid substantial gifts at least, though the decision is really yours in each case. But if you decide to accept any gift, it would be prudent to make quite sure, gently and tactfully, that this is what the client wants you to do. This will help if the client subsequently accuses you of theft, and although such accusations are usually unfounded, they are made.

Defamation

"Defamation is the publication of a statement which tends to lower a person in the estimation of right-thinking members of society generally; or which tends to make them shun or avoid that person."[53] Libel is defamation in written or other permanent form. Slander is defamation in spoken or other transient form. If you make a report which you are required to make, you probably enjoy qualified privilege and can only be sued if malice, or improper motive or spite is proved. Truth and fair comment are always defences. Perhaps the most practical advice is, be scrupulously fair and accurate, and avoid idle tattle.

Witnessing Wills

Suppose you are asked to witness a patient's will. If your employing authority has rules about this, again you should know and observe them. Under the Wills Act 1837, in order to be valid a will must be in writing, must be signed by the maker, called the testator, or by someone else in his presence, and at his direction, signed at the "foot or end" of it and finally signed (or the signature acknowledged) in the presence of two witnesses both present at the same time, and finally signed by the two witnesses. The witnesses customarily add their addresses and occupations. A gift to a witness or his or her spouse is void. The testator must be of sound mind and (unless on active service) over 18.

Certain other legal documents, like deeds, are in practice always witnessed, whether this is required by law or not.

What is most important is that wills are not valid unless they are signed by two witnesses when the testator signs, and much dispute and family argument could be avoided if this were more widely known.

---

53. *Winfield & Jolowicz on Tort*, 9th ed., p 245.

CHAPTER 4

CHILDREN AT LAW

"The Court is placed in a position by reason of the prerogative of the Crown to act as supreme parent of children and must exercise that jurisdiction in the manner in which a wise, affectionate, and careful parent would act for the welfare of the child."
:per Lord Esher M.R. in R. v. Gyngall [1893] 2 Q.B. 232, 241.

THE LEGAL CAPACITY OF CHILDREN

The age of majority since 1970 has been eighteen and when a child reaches that age all parental powers and most orders concerning a child cease, except criminal ones.

A child under ten cannot be convicted of a crime. A child of ten and under 14 is presumed incapable of committing a crime unless it can be shown that the child knew the act was morally wrong. A boy under 14 cannot be convicted of rape or of an offence involving sexual intercourse, whether he knew it was morally wrong or not, but he can be convicted of indecent assault. Over the age of 14, the ordinary rules of law apply, although special provisions apply to sentencing all those under 21.[1] This will be the situation until the Children and Young Persons Act 1969 is fully in force when only care proceedings and prosecutions for homicide (i.e. murder, manslaughter, etc.) will be possible against those under 14.

Minors can sue and be sued just like adults, except that they sue through their "next friend" (usually a parent) and are sued through their guardian *ad litem*. They can sue for all wrongs committed against them, and often for injuries to their person while in the womb.[2] But they can probably sue their parents for assault or negligence.[3] Minority is no defence, but a very young child probably cannot be negligent or contributorily negligent and an older child only so if a child of that age should have been more careful.

Minors can only make contracts to buy "necessaries" (i.e. goods suitable to their position in life and their actual needs on sale and delivery) and contracts for their benefit e.g. apprenticeship and education.

Parents are not answerable at common law for their children's crimes unless guilty of aiding and abetting. But they can be ordered to enter into a recognizance for their child's behaviour and by statute a court can order the parent to pay any fine, costs or compensation imposed on an offender of 14

---

1. Children under 17 are usually tried in a juvenile court. See Chapter 1.
2. Congenital Disabilities (Civil Liability) Act 1976.
3. McCallion v. Dodd [1966] N.Z.L.R. 710 (child injured walking along the road through father's negligence); Ash v. Ash (1698) Comb. 357 (daughter successfully sued mother for assault).

and under 17 unless satisfied that the parent did not conduce to the crime by neglecting the duty of due care and control. The court must do so if the child is under 14. Parents are not liable for their children's wrongdoings, but they may be liable on some other ground, for example the child was their agent (e.g. because they sent the child shopping) or they authorised the wrongdoing. They are also liable for their own negligence like allowing a child to run onto a busy road thus causing an accident. Parents are not liable for their children's contracts unless the child was acting on their orders.

THE RIGHTS AND DUTIES OF THE PARENT

Since 1973 the father and mother have had equal rights of custody of their legitimate child.[4] This carries with it the following rights:
  (a) care and control of the child.
  (b) to choose the child's religious and secular education.
  (c) to inflict moderate and reasonable corporal punishment.[5]
  (d) to consent to lawful medical treatment.
  (e) to the services of a child living with the parent.[6]
  (f) to veto the issue of a passport.
  (g) to consent to the child's marriage – though where this is impracticable or withheld the court may give the necessary consent.[7]
  (h) to give the child the father's surname (or the mother's if illegitimate).
  (i) to consent to adoption or freeing for adoption.
  (j) to appoint a testamentary guardian.
Either parent can exercise the right without the other, unless the other voices disapproval.[8] In case of disagreement either can apply to the court, which must regard the child's welfare as "the first and paramount consideration", the family no longer being the sacrosanct unit. However, both parents must still consent to important matters such as marriage or adoption, and the mother still has exclusive right of custody of an illegitimate child in the absence of a court order (usually sought by the father). The father has no right of custody over an unborn child and thus cannot prevent a lawful abortion by injunction.[9]

Taking children away from their parents or guardian is sometimes a criminal offence.

---

4. Sometimes "custody" is used in a narrow sense to mean *de facto* possession of the child's person and actual care and control. Here it will be used in its wide sense to mean the whole bundle of rights and powers vested in the parent or guardian.
5. The right only applies to parents and those *in loco parentis*, e.g. schools, but not, e.g., elder brothers.
6. The importance of this right is that it gives parents their only common law remedy for interference with their parental rights (e.g. by an abducter).
7. No-one may marry under 16. Indeed it is a criminal offence to have sexual intercourse with a girl under 13, and, generally, to have intercourse with a girl of 13 and under 16.
8. S.1 (1) of the Guardianship Act 1973; S.85 (3) of the Children Act 1975. Presumably a voluntary body with whom the mother leaves her child is not now bound to return the child to the father.
9. Paton v. British Pregnancy Advisory Service Trustees [1979] Q.B. 276.

The right of custody brings with it certain correlative duties. The most important are as follows:

(a) the common law duty to afford physical protection where reasonably to be expected[10] – breach of this duty may lead to a prosecution for assault, manslaughter or murder.

(b) the statutory duty not to do anything wilfully (i.e. intentionally or without caring) which is likely to injure the child physically or mentally, which is given effect to by the various offences under the Children and Young Persons Acts 1933 to 1969. The most important is Section 1 of the 1933 Act which makes it an offence wilfully to assault, ill-treat, neglect, abandon or expose a child, or have this done, in a manner likely to cause unnecessary suffering, or injury to the child's health. This offence includes failure to provide adequate food, clothing, medical aid or lodging or to procure them from the DHSS if the parent or guardian cannot provide them.[11] It can be committed by anyone over 16 who is the child's parent or guardian or is legally liable to maintain the child, or has charge, control or actual possession of the child – such as a school teacher or babysitter over 16.

(c) the common law duty to afford moral protection. There are statutory offences of causing or encouraging the seduction or prostitution of a girl under 16, of having a child between 4 and 16 in a brothel, of allowing a child under 16 to beg, and (except under strict conditions) of allowing children to perform in entertainments.

(d) to educate a child between five and 16.

(e) the common law and statutory duty to maintain the child.[12]

The right of custody can be ended or suspended in five ways:

(a) when the child attains 18.

(b) almost certainly if the child (of either sex) marries under 18.

(c) during military service.

(d) on a parent's death.

(e) under a court order.

Under (a) and (b) the right is gone for ever. Under (c) it is suspended. Under (d) and (e) it is transferred to another.

On the death of either parent, the law provides that the survivor shall be guardian of their legitimate minor children together with any testamentary guardian (see Guardianship p 52).

---

10. e.g. R. v. Shepherd (1862) Le. & Ca. 147, where a girl of 18, already completely independent, died at home in childbirth. Held the mother was under no duty to call a midwife. Contrast R. v. Chattaway (1922) 17 C.A.R. 7, starvation of "helpless" daughter aged 25. Parent held liable.

11. This can include unreasonable refusal to consent to surgery: Oakey v. Jackson [1914] 1 K.B. 216 (refusal of consent to the removal of a child's adenoids).

12. On the breakdown of a marriage this duty may be enforced by a court order for maintenance. And if supplementary benefit is granted for a child under 16 the DHSS can recover it from either or both parents. But anyone responsible for an unmarried child under 16 (or under 19 if receiving full-time secondary education) may claim child benefit. This is paid to the mother where both parents live together.

Generally a parent cannot assign custody and any agreement attempting to do so is void and of no effect. There is an exception if husband and wife agree to separate while married and this is part of the agreement, but it is only enforceable if the court considers it for the child's benefit. However, where there is a dispute, whether between the parents, or between one parent and a stranger (e.g. a testamentary guardian), the court can vary the rights of custody, but must treat the child's welfare as the first and paramount consideration. The court can make a "split order", i.e. giving custody to one parent and actual physical care and control to the other (or leaving custody with both parents). Health visitors should note that medical evidence can be vital on what is in the child's best interests. But other considerations include personality and character of the claimants, age and sex of the children,[13] education (including religious education if important), racial and cultural background, and the child's wishes (though the court may disregard these if clearly coached by one parent or contrary to the child's long-term interests). If, following the order, the child is likely to be removed from England and Wales, the order should be stayed, if an appeal is pending. The Desramault case shows what can happen if this is not done. Also the court may restrict or forbid taking the child abroad in its final order or by interlocutory injunction.

Because the inherent jurisdiction of the High Court derives from the Crown's prerogative powers as *parens patriae* (lit., "parent of the country") and because the proceedings are partly administrative as well as judicial (since the first duty is to protect the child) certain special rules of procedure apply.[14] The judge can (and often does) see the child and each parent in private. The judge may receive a confidential report from the child's guardian *ad litem* (at least where that is the Official Solicitor) and either not show it to the parties at all or only to their legal advisers.[15] Also the court may ask the Official Solicitor (or any other suitable person) to act as guardian *ad litem*,[16] particularly if there is medical evidence not called jointly by both parents,[17] which normally should be.

The right of custody can be enforced by a parent by *habeas corpus*, wardship proceedings or an injunction, but a court will not normally enforce it against the child's will after the so-called age of discretion (14 for boys, 16 for girls).

TRANSFERRING THE PARENTAL RIGHT OF CUSTODY

In cases such as child abuse it is often necessary, in order to protect a child, to remove the child physically from a parent. How can this be done lawfully?

A court order is always needed to transfer the right of custody against a parent's will. Even where the parents consent, a court order is often needed.

---

13. Young and sickly children (particularly girls) tend to go to their mother.
14. These do not apply to a magistrates' court or county court.
15. See esp. Official Solicitor v. K. [1965] A.C. 201. But the judge should not promise not to disclose what the child says, because this would cause grave problems if there is an appeal: H. v. H. [1974] 1 A.E.R. 1145.
16. This also applies to divorce county courts and sometimes to magistrates' courts.
17. B. (M) v. B. (R) [1968] 3 A.E.R. 170, 174.

CARE PROCEEDINGS

A local authority's first duty is to guide, advise and assist in order to keep children out of court and out of care. But what if this fails?

In urgent cases a juvenile court or any magistrate can make a Place of Safety Order. This can be done (at any time of the day or night) where a child is being assaulted, ill-treated or neglected, if certain offences are committed, or if any of conditions (a)–(f) listed under Section 1 Proceedings (see below) apply. Sometimes a police officer can take a child to a place of safety without prior authority. The order must state the time (not exceeding 28 days) within which care proceedings must be brought. If there is no order, it is eight days.

VOLUNTARY RECEPTIONS

A child may be received into care without a court order under Section 2 of the Child Care Act 1980. A local authority must receive a child under 17 who is orphaned or abandoned or whose parents or guardian are too ill (physically or mentally) to provide for that child, if their intervention is needed for the child's welfare. A child may also be received voluntarily, e.g. because a parent is ill. To encourage parents to use this section where necessary, an authority cannot keep a child under Section 2 if any parent or guardian wants that child back. But where the child has been in care for the preceding six months, it is a criminal offence to retake the child without the authority's consent or 28 days notice. This protects the child from psychological damage through being wrenched away from foster parents. Further, if certain conditions are met, the authority can pass a resolution under Section 3 of the 1980 Act to assume parental rights and duties (except to consent to adoption) over the child against a parent's will, provided the child is in care under Section 2. If they do, they must notify a parent whose whereabouts are known unless they obtain written consent to the resolution. The matter can be referred to a juvenile court, if the parent objects. The resolution can stand till the child is 18 or be ended earlier, and a parent can apply for rescission. But it will cease automatically if the child is adopted, freed for adoption or if a guardian is appointed. A local authority has a similar power to vest parental rights and duties in a voluntary organisation in whose care the child is. If they do, similar rights of notification, appeal and annulment apply.

SECTION 1 PROCEEDINGS

Under the Children and Young Persons Act 1969 a local authority must investigate if they think care proceedings are needed and bring them if necessary. They can also be brought by a police officer or the NSPCC. A parent or guardian can ask a local authority to bring care proceedings. If they refuse or do nothing within 28 days, the parent or guardian can apply to the juvenile court to compel proceedings. Care proceedings cannot be brought against a child over 16 or married.

The juvenile court can only make an order if:
(i) at least one of the following conditions is satisfied (the "primary condition"):

49

(a) the child's proper development is being avoidably prevented or neglected or the child's health avoidably impaired or neglected or the child is being ill-treated.

(b) condition (a) probably applies because a court has found it applicable to another child in the same household.

(c) condition (a) probably applies because a member or prospective member of the same household has been convicted of one or more specified offences (i.e. offences against children or sexual offences).

(d) the child is exposed to moral danger. But here the child's background and customs are relevant.[18]

(e) the child is beyond the control of a parent or guardian (e.g. "difficult teenagers" and subnormals).

(f) the child is of compulsory school age and is not receiving efficient and suitable full-time education.[19]

(g) the child is guilty of an offence other than homicide.[19]

(ii) the child needs care and control which will probably not be provided without an order (the "secondary condition").

The court can make one of the following orders:

(a) that the parent or guardian[20] enter into a recognizance to take proper care of the child and exercise proper control over the child.

(b) a supervision order placing the child under the supervision of the local authority or a probation officer. This order must end by the child's eighteenth birthday (except a criminal order). It can require the child to live with a named person, and can give the supervisor certain powers. The supervisor must advise, assist and befriend the child. Application can be made for variation or discharge. Appeal lies to the Crown Court.

(c) a care order committing the child to the care of a local authority. This order will, unless varied, last until 18 or sometimes 19. The authority, the parent or guardian, or the child may apply to the court to discharge the order. Appeal lies to the Crown Court. But the authority must keep the child in care (though not necessarily away from home) so long as the order is in force. While in force it vests all the parental powers and duties in the authority.[21]

(d) a hospital order under the Mental Health Act 1959 (see p 41).

(e) a guardianship order under the same Act (see *ibid*).

An interim order can be made, and has the same effect as the full order.

The local authority looks after every child in care. They must ascertain and consider the child's wishes and feelings given the age and understanding of that child. But if the child was placed in care by the High Court in any proceedings, or a county court in matrimonial proceedings, the court making

---

18. Mohamed v. Knott [1969] 1 Q.B. 1 (where it was held that a Nigerian girl of 13 was not exposed to moral danger merely because she was having sexual intercourse with a man aged 26 to whom she was validly married under Nigerian law).

19. These can only be brought by a local authority or, in the case of (g), a police officer.

20. Or a child, who is over 14, consents and has been found guilty of an offence.

21. S.10 (1) & (2) of the Child Care Act 1980.

the order retains overriding control. Each parent must normally pay full maintenance according to a set scale until the child is 16, though the local authority can mitigate this. If a parent refuses, the court can make a contribution order to compel payment.

If a child in care is placed with foster parents they must normally return the child whenever the authority so demands.[22] Where a child is in care, the court tends not to interfere with the authority's discretion. But the court will always intervene if they break their duty, act *ultra vires* or follow an improper procedure, or if their powers need supplementing.

WARDSHIP

Historically the wardship jurisdiction of the High Court derives from the Crown's prerogative powers as *parens patriae*. Today it is dealt with by the Family Division. If a child is a ward of court the right of custody is taken over by the court. Care and control are given to an individual, who must keep the court informed of the ward's progress and can turn to it for guidance and assistance. But the court makes all major decisions, e.g. access, education and marriage.

Wilful interference with the ward or guardian is contempt of court, as is disobedience by the ward. It is also contempt for a ward to marry (or even attempt to marry) without the court's consent. Indeed it is probably prudent to obtain the court's consent to other than routine medical treatment or surgery.

The wardship jurisdiction is useful in many situations, for example where someone other than a parent (such as a health visitor or social worker) wishes to bring a child before the court because perhaps neither parent is fit to have custody. In one case a social worker warded a mentally retarded girl of 11 to prevent her permanent sterilization, though her mother had consented.[23] In another, a local authority warded a new-born mongol girl and the Court of Appeal ordered an operation (against the parents' wishes) to remove an intestinal blockage and preserve her life, because the court considered it in her best interests.[24]

The advantage of wardship is often that the parents have care and control, but the court is in constant supervision. But it can also be used e.g. to prevent a teenage girl from associating with undesirable companions or marrying against her parents' wishes, or to prevent a child being kidnapped and taken out of the country. It is sometimes used in divorce proceedings.

A child can only become a ward of court by a court order. But immediately an order is applied for, the child becomes a ward, though this ceases unless an appointment to hear the summons is obtained within 21 days or if the court

---

22. In re A.B. [1954] 2 Q.B. 385 where the court ordered the foster-parents to return the child. The agreement which foster-parents are required to sign under the Boarding-Out of Children Regulations 1955 includes an undertaking to permit the authority to remove the child.
23. In re D [1976] F 185.
24. In re B [1981] 1 W.L.R. 1421.

refuses to make the order. In an emergency a judge can make a temporary order at any time of the day or night.

In wardship proceedings, the court can appoint a guardian *ad litem* for the child, usually the Official Solicitor. It always does in disputes between parent and a "teenage" child. A ward may be placed in local authority care or under the supervision of a welfare officer or local authority. But either parent of a legitimate child may be ordered to pay maintenance.

Wardship ceases if the court so orders and anyway at 18. But it does not cease on marriage.

GUARDIANSHIP

A guardian is someone who voluntarily stands *in loco parentis* (i.e. in place of the parent) to a ward (i.e. the child). At common law, parents are the child's natural guardians, though in common parlance the concepts of parent and guardian are distinct and they are kept distinct here. A legal guardian may be appointed by deed or will (a "testamentary guardian") or by the court and has the legal rights and duties discussed above (see p 45ff).[25] Guardianship generally ends on death, majority and possibly the marriage of the ward, though the High Court can remove a guardian if the ward's welfare so demands.

FOSTER PARENTS

Foster parents do not have the right of custody, but mere *de facto* control of the child. Their position is precarious but common, whether as grandparents or other relatives, who just "take over" where both parents die, or as local authority foster parents. If their title is disputed the court must be guided by the child's welfare. If it is not disputed they retain the child. They owe a duty at common law and under the 1933 Act to protect the child and they commit an offence under that Act if they wilfully fail to provide adequate food, clothing, medical aid or lodging. They must also ensure the child receives full-time education.

Anyone other than a guardian, custodian, adult relative or local or public authority who undertakes the permanent care and maintenance of a child (with or without payment) is now subject to the Foster Children Act 1980. This Act requires periodic visits by the social services department to inspect and advise, but does not apply to adopted children or children under a supervision order. But anyone proposing to maintain a foster child must notify the local authority, which has certain powers of inspection and control, subject to an appeal to the juvenile court.

CUSTODIANSHIP

This is where the court gives the right of custody to someone other than the parents, and is designed particularly to help the precarious position of foster

---

25. The main difference is that a guardian must ensure the ward receives the religious education the parents would have wished.

52

parents. The relevant powers are contained in Part II of the Children Act 1975, which was not yet in force when this book went to press.

Three categories of people may apply. (a) A relative or step-parent, provided the child's home was with them for the three months before the application and the person with legal custody consents. (b) Anyone, provided the child's home was with them for a total of at least twelve months including the three months before the application and the person with legal custody consents. (c) Anyone, provided the child's home was with them for a total of at least three years including the three months before the application.

The three month rule enables the local authority to ensure that the child is likely to settle. The consent rule prevents foster parents being able to apply automatically thus jeopardizing the whole fostering system. But where no-one has legal custody, or the applicant has it, or where the person who has it cannot be found, consent is not required. More than one person may apply, and though they are usually husband and wife they need not be, e.g. two sisters can apply. Parents, however, cannot apply, nor can a step-parent if the child was named as a child of the family in previous divorce or nullity proceedings.

A custodianship order can be made by the High Court, a county court or a magistrates' court. Within seven days of the application the applicant must notify the local authority in whose area the child resides and an officer of that authority must report to the court.[26] The court can require a report independently. Once the application is made no-one may remove the child from the applicant's custody without the applicant's consent or the court's leave, provided the child's home was there for a total of at least three years. This protects the applicant, who might otherwise be afraid to apply.

While a custodianship order is in force, the right of custody is generally given to the custodian and the right of anyone else to custody is suspended. But the parent or guardian retains certain powers: e.g. to consent to marriage or adoption, and to appoint a guardian. Also the court can order access and/or maintenance. Since people with whom children are boarded out by a local authority are paid and may well not be able to afford custodianship without that allowance, authorities can, where appropriate, contribute to the cost of accommodation and maintenance, provided the custodian is not the spouse of the child's parent.

A custodianship order can be revoked on the application of the custodian, the child's parent or guardian, or a local authority. But to protect custodians from harassment by parents, no-one may re-apply for revocation after a previous unsuccessful application without the court's leave. Unless the court otherwise orders, revocation revives the rights of whoever would have been entitled to custody without the order. But the court must ascertain who this is, and if necessary commit the child to local authority care or to the supervision of the authority or a probation officer. One of these orders can also be made on the initial application.

---

26. The matters to be covered are prescribed by regulations.

ADOPTION

Adoption severs for ever the legal ties between child and natural parent and the adoptive parent stands in all respects in the shoes of the natural parent towards the child.

The law on this subject is being amended by the Children Act 1975, in provisions not yet fully in force when we went to press (March 1982). The Adoption Act 1958 (the present Act) and the changes to it are to be consolidated in the Adoption Act 1976 (also not yet in force). The new law will provide a comprehensive adoption service called "the Adoption Service" to work through local authorities and now prevents "private adoptions" by making it illegal for anyone other than an adoption agency to place a child for, or otherwise arrange, an adoption unless the proposed adopter is a relative or acts under a High Court order.

Only one person or a married couple can apply for adoption, and each parent or guardian of the child must agree. Sometimes, however, this consent can be dispensed with, especially where the parent or guardian is not available, unreasonably withholds consent or neglects or ill-treats the child.

The new law will enable the court to make an order freeing a child for adoption which will allow the adoption to proceed without further consent of the parents or guardian. This will save prospective adopters the worry that consent may be withdrawn at the last minute.

Prospective adopters must have had continuous actual custody of the child after the age of six weeks and for at least three months before the order is made.[27] This ensures their suitability so far as possible. They must also give the local authority, where the child's home was, three months' written notice if the child is below the upper limit of compulsory school age. This ensures proper supervision.

The court must appoint a guardian *ad litem* for the child, usually the Official Solicitor (in the High Court) or the Director of Social Services or a probation officer (in other courts). The guardian *ad litem* must conduct various enquiries and interviews and make a confidential report to the court, which in the High Court at least the parties may not see without the court's leave.[28] Under the new law a guardian *ad litem* will not always be needed, and the report can be made by the adoption agency or local authority.

The adoption order can be made by the High Court, a county court or a magistrates' court. In practice most are made by county courts. The court must be satisfied of three things. (a) That each parent or guardian of the child agrees freely, unconditionally and with full understanding (unless consent has been dispensed with). (b) That no unauthorised payments or rewards have been made or agreed on. (c) That the order will be for the child's welfare (the report is important here). The court can impose any terms it thinks fit, supported if necessary by an undertaking to the court.

---

27. Under the new law the periods will be thirteen weeks and nineteen weeks respectively, and additional safeguards are provided.
28. In re P.A. [1971] 3 A.E.R. 522 *per* Lord Denning M.R.

If an adoption order is refused, a supervision order or a care order may in exceptional circumstances be made.

AFFILIATION

Affiliation proceedings are brought in a magistrates' court under the Affiliation Proceedings Act 1957 by the mother of an illegitimate child or by the DHSS to determine that child's paternity. The mother must have been single at the child's birth or at the time of application. Proceedings may be brought by consent to give the child a stable pedigree, but usually they seek a maintenance order against the putative father. This can only be made if paternity is proved. Blood tests can be made if each party consents, though the court can draw adverse inferences if consent is refused. They can never prove paternity, but sometimes they exclude or indicate probable paternity.

DOMESTIC VIOLENCE

Under the Domestic Violence and Matrimonial Proceedings Act 1976 either spouse can seek an injunction in the county court preventing the other from molesting the applicant or any child living with the applicant, and/or excluding the other from all or part of the matrimonial home, or its environs. Where violence has occurred and is likely to recur, the court can (and usually does) attach a power of arrest enabling the police to arrest and detain the other spouse, but it should give reasons for doing so. "Molesting" includes mere pestering or annoying as well as assaulting. And this Act applies to those unmarried but co-habiting, though not to divorcees. There is a similar procedure for obtaining this type of injunction in the High Court.

Under the Domestic Proceedings and Magistrates' Courts Act 1978 magistrates have similar though less extensive powers. Where one spouse has used violence against the other or a child of the family, or has used actual violence against someone else and has threatened violence against the applicant or the child, a magistrates' court can order that spouse not to do so. And if there is imminent physical danger the court can exclude them from the matrimonial home. The order may also forbid that spouse inciting or assisting anyone else to use or threaten violence. And again the court can (and usually does) attach a power of arrest, but again it should give reasons.

DIVORCE

Custody, maintenance and access on a divorce are a matter for the divorce court and are outside the scope of this book. Health visitors should note, however, that the divorce court can make a care or supervision order and can make a child of the family a ward of court. It may also receive a welfare report on a child and in exceptional circumstances appoint a guardian *ad litem*.

MISCELLANEOUS

On the application of either parent under the Guardianship of Minors Act 1971 (including either parent of an illegitimate child) the High Court, a county court or a magistrates' court can give all or some of the rights of custody to one parent only. The order can provide for maintenance for a legitimate child. An order can also be made for access by either parent or a grandparent. At present custody can also be given to a third party, but this will eventually be replaced by a custodianship order (see p 52). In exceptional circumstances a supervision order or a care order can be made under this Act.

The 1978 Act enables a magistrates' court to make maintenance orders for a "child of the family" – i.e. any child under 18 (legitimate or illegitimate) born to or adopted by both parties or treated by them as a child of their family (but excluding children boarded out by a local authority or voluntary organisation). Either spouse can apply. It also enables a magistrates' court to give custody of a child of the family to either spouse or to a parent if not the child of them both. Access can be given to either spouse, a parent or a grandparent. But the court can only give custody to one person, though it may leave some rights jointly with both spouses. If so, and there is a dispute, either can apply to the court. Eventually, the court will be able to give custody to a third party by making a custodianship order (see p 52). In exceptional circumstances the court can make a care order (which may provide for maintenance) or a supervision order under this Act. The court can call for a report from a probation officer or the Director of Social Services.

CHAPTER 5

THE CORONER

The work of the health visitor is devoted to the preservation and amelioration of human life. But all human life must one day perish, and when it does sometimes a coroner's inquest must be held. This is the subject of our final chapter.

1. The office of coroner and its function: "This is a very ancient and important office in the realm of England".[1] The office of coroner goes back certainly to the early thirteenth century and possibly to Anglo-Saxon times. It is so called because of the duties of coroners in relation to "pleas of the crown" *(placita coronae)* in medieval times.

Today coroners must be appointed for each county by the County Council, for Greater London by the GLC and for the City of London and the Inner and Middle Temples by the Common Council of the City of London. If, as often happens, the county is divided into districts each will have a separate coroner. Coroners must be barristers, solicitors or legally qualified medical practitioners, in each case of five years' standing. Every coroner must appoint a deputy and may appoint an assistant deputy, both similarly qualified.

Coroners' jurisdiction is generally limited to the area for which they are appointed. But a coroner for a district is for all purposes a coroner for the whole county, though such coroners can only hold an inquest in another district in cases of illness, incapacity, unavoidable absence or vacancy in the office of coroner for that district. But the place of death or where the cause of death arose are irrelevant, and a coroner has jurisdiction if the body is lying within that coroner's area. And this can be important where death occurred at sea, in the air or abroad.

A coroner has four functions: 1) to inquire into deaths by holding an inquest or by having a post-mortem examination made; 2) to hold inquests on treasure trove; 3) to act for the sheriff; and 4) in the City of London to hold inquests on fires. Here we are only concerned with the inquiry into deaths.

2. A death occurs: Where a coroner is informed that the dead body of a person is lying within that coroner's jurisdiction, and there are reasonable grounds to suspect that they died either violently or unnaturally, or suddenly without known cause, or in prison or in a place or in circumstances which require an inquest under any Act, then there must be an inquest. Where death is sudden without known cause, the coroner may have a post-mortem examination made without holding an inquest if the coroner thinks that will make an inquest unnecessary. Where death is violent, unnatural or sudden without known cause, the coroner has the right and duty at common law to take and keep possession of the body until after the inquest, though there is a discretion to order an earlier release which is often used in practice.

It is the duty of everyone to furnish any information which may lead the coroner to learn of circumstances in which an inquest must be held. In

1. In re Ward (1861) 30 L.J. Ch 775 *per* Lord Campbell L.C.

particular, if a Registrar of Births and Deaths is informed of a death within twelve months, then the registrar must report it to the coroner *inter alia* if the deceased was not attended during any final illness by a doctor or was not seen by the certifying doctor either after death or within fourteen days before. But this could also place a health visitor under a duty to report a death to the coroner.

All deaths must be registered with the Registrar of Births and Deaths within five days. A doctor who has attended a person during their last illness must send the registrar a medical certificate stating the cause of death to the best of the doctor's knowledge and belief, but in cases of doubt or suspicion the death is normally reported to the coroner, though this is not required by law. The doctor will also give the person required to inform the registrar of the death (usually a relative) notice of signing the certificate which that person must take to the registrar, unless there is to be an inquest. The registrar must then register the death and issue a death certificate and a disposal certificate authorising the funeral to proceed. For cremation two doctors' signatures and extra forms are needed. But where the matter is referred to the coroner the funeral cannot normally proceed until a burial order or cremation certificate (as appropriate) is issued by the coroner. This may have to await the conclusion of any inquest, but that is a matter for the coroner. It is illegal to dispose of a body without a registrar's certificate or coroner's order.

A coroner has no absolute right to hold an inquest, and any coroner who tries to do so without reasonable cause can be restrained by a writ of *Prohibition* from the Queen's Bench Division.[2] If, therefore, a doctor has signed or is willing to sign a medical certificate and there are no circumstances appearing to demand an inquest or post-mortem examination, the coroner, if informed of the death, should notify the Registrar of Births and Deaths that an inquest is not considered necessary.

A coroner has no jurisdiction over a foetus expelled before separate existence is possible, nor (unless there is doubt whether separate existence has been achieved) over a still birth.

If, however, there is no body (for example because it has been destroyed by fire or is irrecoverable, e.g. in a mining disaster) the coroner may report the facts to the Secretary of State who can direct an inquest.

When appropriate, jurisdiction can be transferred from one coroner to another. This is useful, for example, where several people have been killed in a railway or colliery disaster and taken to different hospitals, and it is better for one coroner to hold an inquest on all the fatalities. In such cases the coroner usually holds the inquests on each deceased concurrently.

If the coroner directs a post-mortem examination which reveals that death was due to natural causes and nothing indicates the desirability of a public inquiry, and the coroner is satisfied that an inquest is unnecessary, then the coroner must notify the Registrar of Births and Deaths accordingly and issue a burial order or cremation certificate. Examinations are usually conducted by

---

2. See R. v. Price (1884) 12 Q.B.D. 247, 248 "It would be intolerable if [the coroner] had power to intrude without adequate cause upon the privacy of a family in distress and to inerefere with their arrangements for a funeral" *per* Stephen J.

experienced pathologists. If anyone states on oath before the coroner that they believe the death was caused partly or wholly by improper or negligent treatment by a doctor or by someone else, then that practitioner or other person has the right to be represented at any post-mortem examination. This could include a health visitor. Where a legally qualified medical practitioner conducts an examination, the coroner must (unless it is impracticable or would unduly delay the examination) inform certain people or bodies of its time and place. These include any relative of the deceased who has notified the coroner of their desire to attend or be represented, the deceased's regular medical attendant, and the hospital, if any, where the death occurred. Any of these can be represented at the examination by a legally qualified medical practitioner, or may attend in person if they are one. The coroner has a discretion to inform anyone of the time and place of the examination and to allow them to attend. The person conducting the examination must report to the coroner but may not supply a copy of the report to anyone else without the coroner's authority.

3. The inquest: The inquest itself must be in public, unless the coroner considers that in the interests of national security it should be partly or wholly in private. A jury is only required in five cases specified by statute: (a) where murder, manslaughter or infanticide are suspected; (b) for deaths in prison or where the inquest is required under an Act of Parliament (other than the Coroners Act 1887); (c) where there was an accident, poisoning or disease which has to be notified to a particular government authority (e.g. factory and railway accidents); (d) where there was an accident involving a vehicle on a public road; (e) where the circumstances could recur and endanger public health or safety.

The inquest is opened by proclamation or other formal manner. If there is a jury, the list of jurors is called over and the jury sworn. The coroner has power under Section 4 of the Coroners Act 1980 to order the exhumation of a body in order to hold the inquest. Coroners are no longer obliged to view the body, though they (and presumably any jury) can still do so.[3]

Coroners' proceedings are inquisitorial and not, as in the ordinary courts, adversarial. They ask, "Why did this man die?" and not, "Is this man guilty or not guilty?" or "Is the plaintiff or the defendant in the right?" There is no plaintiff or defendant. The coroner conducts the inquest, and examines the witnesses in chief. But all those who wish to give evidence or who have knowledge of the facts and whom the coroner thinks it expedient to examine must be examined. And anyone whose conduct is, in the coroner's opinion, likely to be called into question at the inquest must either be summoned or be given reasonable notice of the inquest. This could include a health visitor. Also anyone who, in the coroner's opinion, is properly interested, is entitled to examine any witness either personally or by counsel or solicitor. This too could include a health visitor. The Health Visitors' Association recommends that if health visitors have to give evidence at an inquest and there is any possibility of their work being called in question in any way, they should be supported by a Legal Officer (see p 15). And since Legal Aid is not yet available in

3. S.1 of the Coroners Act 1980.

proceedings before coroners, the Association may be willing to pay for representation if necessary. The coroner has the power to summon witnesses.

The coroner must notify the date, hour and place of an inquest to the spouse or a near relative, executor or administrator of the deceased whose name and address are known to the coroner, and to anyone whose act or omission may in the coroner's opinion caused or contributed to the death, provided that person has asked to be notified and has supplied an address or telephone number. This could include a health visitor.

Evidence is given on oath as in the ordinary courts. But unless the coroner decides otherwise, witnesses must be examined by the coroner first and by their own representative (if any) last. If several people are entitled to cross-examine witnesses, the coroner must decide the order after consulting all the interested parties. In the case of every inquest held the coroner may record all material evidence in depositions which must be signed by both coroner and witness. Normally the depositions should be read over, though this is not essential. If depositions are not taken, the coroner must take notes of the evidence. The strict laws of evidence do not apply, though in practice they are usually followed, especially in cases of murder, manslaughter or infanticide. In particular, a witness is not bound to answer any question which may incriminate them, and the coroner must disallow any question which in the coroner's opinion is irrelevant or improper.

If the coroner is informed before the jury give their verdict that someone has been charged before the magistrates with the deceased's murder, manslaughter or infanticide, or with causing the death by reckless driving, or with aiding, abetting, counselling or procuring the deceased's suicide, the coroner must generally adjourn the inquest until the criminal proceedings have concluded. Also, if any person's conduct is called into question at an inquest and the coroner considers the grounds substantial and the criticism relevant to the inquest, it must be adjourned to enable that person to attend, unless they have already been summoned or otherwise notified.

If a majority of the jury consider the cause of death has not been satisfactorily explained by the evidence before them they may require the coroner in writing to summon as a witness a legally qualified medical practitioner named by them and to direct that practitioner to conduct a post-mortem examination, even if an examination has already been made. The coroner must comply.

The proceedings and evidence at an inquest must be directed solely to ascertaining who the deceased was and how, when and where the death occurred. No speeches are allowed concerning the facts either to the coroner or the jury. Where there is a jury, the coroner must sum up the evidence to them and direct them on the law before they consider their verdict. When the verdict is returned, either by the coroner or by the jury, it must be certified by an inquisition in writing stating, so far as has been proved, who the deceased was, and how, when and where the death occurred.

Finally the inquest must be formally closed, and the coroner must send the Registrar of Births and Deaths a certificate of the findings.

The Queen's Bench Division has power to control procedings before a coroner. Where appropriate it may prevent the inquest proceeding by a writ of *Prohibition* or quash the inquisition afterwards by *Certiorari*. It may also order a fresh inquest, or order an inquest to be held where none has been held in the first place.

APPENDICES

Appendix I

FORMS OF ADDRESS FOR THE JUDICIARY IN COURT

High Court Judges:[1]

Verbal address:	My Lord or Your Lordship[2]
	(My Lady or Your Ladyship)[2]
Description in conversation:	His Lordship (Her Ladyship)
Description in writing:	The Hon. Mr (Mrs) Justice Blackstone

Circuit Judges:[1]

Verbal address:	Your Honour[3]
Description in conversation:	His (Her) Honour
Description in writing:	His (Her) Honour Judge Jefferys

Recorders:[1]

Verbal Address:	Your Honour[3]
Description in conversation:	His (Her) Honour
Description in writing:	Mr (Mrs) Recorder Bracton

Magistrates:[1]

Verbal Address:	Your Worship[4]
Description in conversation:	His (Her) Worship or Their Worships[5]
Description in writing:	A. Littleton, Esq., JP[6]
	Mrs (Miss/title) A. Glanvil, JP[6]

Coroners:

Verbal address:	Sir (Madam)
Description in conversation:	The Coroner
Description in Writing:	Dr Lister (or as appropriate)

Registrars of the County Court & Family Division:[1]

Verbal address:	Sir (Madam)
Description in conversation:	The Registrar
Description in writing:	Mr (Mrs/Miss/title) Registrar Coke

The above should suffice for most if not all the professional needs of the health visitor. For the superior courts the matter is regulated by Practice Directions which are issued from time to time (the present one being [1982] 1 W.L.R. 101), but further advice can normally be found in *Debrett's Correct Form*, Part IV, "Styles by Office" – "Legal Section", or from *Titles & Forms of Address* (published by A. & C. Black).

1. As to which judges sit in which courts see p 12ff. Normally the court in which a judge sits will tell you the appropriate style of address. If not (as in the Crown Court), then look at the judge's name on the list outside court (see p 17) and that will determine the matter conclusively.
2. "My Lord" is used when addressing the judge in the second person, e.g. "Yes, my Lord", "your Lordship" when addressing the judge in the third person, e.g. "If your Lordship pleases".
3. All judges at the Central Criminal Court (i.e. the Old Bailey) are addressed as "My Lord" etc., including those who are only circuit judges and thus styled in writing "His (Her) Honour Judge Jeffreys". This rule also applies to the Honorary Recorder of Liverpool, the Honorary Recorder of Manchester, the judge of the Mayor's and City of London Court (which though only a county court is technically part of the Old Bailey) and any circuit judge sitting as a deputy High Court judge. The rule also applies to Recorders sitting at the Old Bailey.
4. Counsel alone are allowed to address magistrates as "Sir" ("Madam").
5. Sometimes the expression "the learned magistrate" is used of stipendiary magistrates as they are all qualified barristers or solicitors (see p 14).
6. The letters "J.P." are not used for stipendiary magistrates, because they are not J.P.s.

64

CASES OF PARTICULAR RELEVANCE TO HEALTH VISITORS

Chapter 2:

a) Contemporaneous Record:

R. v. Simmonds (1967) 51 C.A.R. 316, 329f. Customs officers made up their notes immediately on return to their offices from long and complicated interviews. HELD (by the Court of Appeal) that whether a note is "contemporaneous" is "a matter of fact and degree". Here the notes were contemporaneous having been prepared at the first available opportunity. The court said that this was fairer and more sense than the officers having to memorise by heart long and complicated interviews.

Horne v. Mackenzie (1839) 6 Cl. & Fin 628. A surveyor made a report for his employers and was then called as a witness. He produced a printed copy of his report (with a few marginal jottings added two days before the trial). The report (except the jottings) was made up from his original notes of which it was in substance, though not verbatim, a transcript. HELD (by the House of Lords) that he could refresh his memory from it.

R. v. Cheng (1976) 63 C.A.R. 20. Policeman's notebook not available at trial, but he had transcribed in statement form what was in the notebook, omitting certain irrelevant entries. HELD (by the Court of Appeal) that he could refresh his memory from it. The court said "If the statement in this case, or any other transcription of notes in other cases, is substantially what is in the notes and there is evidence to that effect, then the judge should allow the witness to refresh his memory from the statement or transcription as the case may be. But if, after investigation, it turns out that the statement or transcription bears little relation to the original note, then . . . the judge in the exercise of his discretion would be entitled to refuse to allow a witness to refresh his memory from such an imperfect source of information."

b) Confidentiality:

D v. NSPCC [1977] 2 W.L.R. 201. The NSPCC received a complaint about a 14 month old girl. An inspector called. The mother was most upset and called the family doctor who said there was nothing wrong with the child. The mother sued for damages for negligence and sought the name of the informant. HELD (by the House of Lords) that the name should not be disclosed. NB It seems that their Lordships were in some measure influenced by the fact that the society has a statutory power to bring care proceedings under Section 1 of the Children and Young Persons Act 1969.

In re D (Infants) [1970] 1 W.L.R. 599. Two children in care were boarded out with foster parents. The mother sought custody and the County Council and the foster parents sought to have them made wards of court. During cross-examination of the Council's child care officer, counsel for the mother sought disclosure of the case records kept by the County Council under Regulation 10 of the Boarding-Out of Children Regulations 1955. HELD (by the Court of Appeal) that the records were confidential and could not be disclosed. Lord Denning M.R. said he had never known discovery ordered in a custody case, and he did not intend to start now. Harman & Karminski L.J.J. agreed.

In re a Complaint against Liverpool City Council [1977] 1 W.L.R. 995. A child in care was boarded out with foster parents, then removed from care. The foster parents complained of maladministration by the local authority. The Local Commissioner (the local "Ombudsman") sought production of the records made by the local authority under Regulation 10 (as above). HELD (by the Divisional Court of the Queen's Bench Division) that the records could not be produced because Section 32 (3) of the Local Government Act 1974 provides that if a minister or local authority gives the Local Commissioner notice that in their opinion disclosure of any document would be injurious to the public interest, such documents shall not be produced unless the Secretary of State discharges the notice. Such notice had been served here and not discharged, so the documents could not be disclosed. The court, though, expressly left undecided whether if the Secretary of State did discharge the notice, the common law position established in In re D (Infants) (supra) would on balance apply. But Lord Widgery C.J. did say that that case showed "the courts recognise as being within the public interest that these very records should be maintained on a confidential basis." Michael Davies and Robert Goff J.J. agreed.

A.-G. v. Mulholland [1963] 2 Q.B. 477, 489, where Lord Denning M.R. said "Take the clergyman, the banker or the medical man. None of these is entitled to refuse to answer when directed to by a judge. Let me not be mistaken. The judge will respect the confidences which each member of these honourable professions receives in the course of it, and will not direct him to answer unless not only it is relevant but also it is a proper and, indeed, necessary question in the course of justice to be put and answered. A judge is the person entrusted, on behalf of the community, to weigh these conflicting interests – to weigh on the one hand the respect due to confidence in the profession and on the other hand the ultimate interest of the community in justice being done."

R. v. Birmingham City Council, Ex parte O. [1982] 1 W.L.R. 679. Foster parents applied to adopt one of their foster children. The social services department was agreeable in principle. A councillor not on the social services committee discovered amongst other things that the husband had been in prison and asked to see the files concerning the adoption. HELD (by a majority of the Court of Appeal) that the files were confidential and could not be disclosed to the councillor.

N.B. When we went to press this case was subject to an appeal to the House of Lords.

c) Negligence:

Roe v. Minister of Health [1954] 2 Q.B. 66. An anaesthetist used nupercaine which had been stored in phenol in sealed glass ampoules. The phenol had seeped through invisible cracks or molecular flaws into the nupercaine and the patient developed spastic paraplegia. HELD (by the Court of Appeal) that the anaesthetist was not negligent because the operation took place in 1947 and the attention of the profession was only drawn to this risk in 1951.

Evans v. London Hospital Medical College (University of London) [1981] 1 W.L.R. 184. Post mortem and toxological investigations were carried out on a five-month old boy. Reports were made and the mother was prosecuted for murder. The reports were inaccurate and the prosecution was dropped. HELD (by Drake J.) that just as witnesses cannot be guilty of negligence for the evidence they give, so also those who prepare statements or reports to facilitate civil or criminal proceedings cannot be guilty of negligence for those statements or reports.

McKay v. Essex Area Health Authority [1982] 2 W.L.R. 890. An expectant mother contracted rubella and her child was born disabled. Mother and child sued the Health Authority and the doctor for negligence. HELD (by the Court of Appeal) that although a doctor could lawfully advise and help to effect an abortion under the Abortion Act 1967, there was no legal obligation to terminate the life of a foetus because that would violate the sanctity of human life. Thus there was no question of the doctor being negligent on that ground.

N.B. The decision in this case is reinforced by the Congenital Disabilities (Civil Liability) Act 1976.

litigation.

Blackacre   A term used by lawyers for an imaginary piece of land.

Certiorari   An order of the Divisional Court to remove a case from an inferior court or tribunal for a fairer trial or to remove an error (lit. "to be made more sure").

Counsel   A barrister.

De facto   Actual, if not rightful.

Defendant   The person against whom a civil action (or sometimes a prosecution) is brought.

Habeas corpus   An order of the Divisional Court to one who detains another to produce (lit. "have the body") of that other in court, to effect their release.

Injunction   A court order commanding someone to do something, or, more usually, not to do it. An injunction granted before a full trial is called an "interlocutory injunction".

In loco parentis   In place of the parent.

In re   In the matter of.

Minor   Under the Family Law Reform Act 1969 those under 18 may be styled at law "minors" instead of the older term "infants".

Moot   A form of mock trial for law students, especially at the Inns of Court. From the Anglo-Saxon word *Gemot* meaning "meeting" or "court".

Per   Said by (a judge).

Plaintiff   The person bringing a civil action.

Prohibition   An order of the Divisional Court restraining an inferior court or tribunal from proceeding with a case.

Recognizance   A secured promise or undertaking to the court.

Royal Prerogative   The residuary powers recognised at common law as belonging solely to the Crown, e.g. to dissolve Parliament, pardon criminals and appoint honours.

Tort   A civil wrong giving a right to sue for damages, and sometimes an injunction.

Ultra vires   Beyond one's power or authority.

Tortfeasor   The person committing a Tort.

Young Person   Under the Children And Young Persons Act 1969 this is someone of 14 and under 17, while a "child" is generally someone under 14. "Child" in this book has its ordinary sense.

:   This colon is used by lawyers to show that the case or statute following is the legal source and authority for what has just been said.

ABBREVIATIONS

ACAS   Advisory Conciliation and Arbitration Service.

CA   Court of Appeal.

CJ   Chief Justice.

DHSS   Department of Health and Social Security.

DoE   Department of Employment

EEC   European Economic Community.

GLC   Greater London Council.

GP   General Practitioner.

HL   House of Lords.

J   e.g. Blackstone J. – the Hon. Mr Justice Blackstone (a High Court judge).

JP   Justice of the Peace.

KB   King's Bench.

LC   Lord Chancellor

LJ(J)   Lord(s) Justice(s) (judges of the Court of Appeal).

MR   Master of the Rolls.

NHS   National Health Service.

NSPCC   National Society for the Prevention of Cruelty to Children.

PAYE   Pay as you Earn (income tax).

QB   Queen's Bench.

QC   Queen's Counsel.

S   Section (of an Act).

SI   Statutory Instrument.

SR & O   Statutory Rule and Order (an old name for Statutory Instruments).

TUC   Trades Union Congress.

v   versus.

Note – The abbreviations in the citation of Law Reports can be found in Sweet & Maxwell's *Where to Look for your Law.*

INDEX

71